Wife after God

Drawing Closer to God & Your Husband

A 30-Day Marriage Devotional by

Unveiled Wife

JENNIFER SMITH

- Second Edition -

Wife After God

Drawing Closer To God & Your Husband

- *Second Edition* -

Written By: Jennifer Smith
Formatted By: Aaron Smith
Cover Art By: Jane Johnson

ISBN-10: 0-9863667-4-9
ISBN-13: 978-0-9863667-4-1
LCCN: 2016902872

WifeAfterGod.com || UnveiledWife.com
Facebook.com/unveiledwife
Pinterest.com/unveiledwife
Twitter.com/unveiledwife

Give feedback on the book at:
WifeAfterGod.com

Printed in U.S.A

Disclaimer: *The content in this devotional although rooted in Biblical principles are the expressed interpretations and opinions of Aaron & Jennifer Smith. We are not licensed professionals. There are certain situations in a marriage that may need the assistance of professionals or authorities, such as abuse. Please do not hesitate to seek professional help.*

This devotional is dedicated to my amazing husband. Thank you for encouraging me, supporting me, and always pointing me to Christ. I love you!

This devotional is also dedicated to Gary And Courtney. Thank you for showing me how to step out in faith. Your friendship is priceless!

WHAT OTHER WIVES ARE SAYING

"I love this devotional and her style of writing -it is so warm, comforting and inspiring. If you need someone to come along side you and gently lead you as a wife - this book will do just that for you."
Courtney Joseph / womenlivingwell.org

"Every word in her devotional reflects God, His Word and His love story with humanity. She brings Godly wisdom and clarification to controversial topics like submission. I can't recommend this devotional highly enough; it cuts to the core of marriage which starts with a daily, intimate relationship with the first lover of our souls, Jesus Christ."
Selena Fredrick / FierceMarriage.com

"This is an excellent devotional for any wife who was seeking to grow in her spiritual walk and in her marriage. It is deep and rich, yet presented in these nice, short "bites" so that each chapter is just enough encouragement and challenge for that day. Jennifer asks some terrific questions at the end of every chapter and includes a lovely prayer too. Highly recommend!"
Lisa Jacobson / club31women.com

"In the pursuit to love your husband emotionally, spiritually and physically, which is the very essence of intimacy, its easy to get sidetrucked in the minutia of everyday life. "Wife After God" will inspire you to intentionally pray for your husband and cultivate deeper intimacy with each other and God."
Trisha Davis author of Beyond Ordinary; When a Good Marriage Isn't Good Enough.

"Wife After God is not merely a good book, but a transforming journey. I picked it up expecting to read about the marriage relationship, but each devotion taught me something profound about the Lord and what it means to be a cherished daughter of the Most High. Jennifer Smith understands, teaches, and encourages the reader to draw close to the Author of love in order to have a more intimate marriage with her husband. One cannot complete this book and remain unchanged. Personally, I grew in my relationship with the Lord and thus grew in my relationship with my husband. My marriage and my walk with the Lord benefited from this well-written

devotional. I highly recommend to everyone (even single women)."
Darby Dugger / darbydugger.com

"Wife After God is a great resource for wives who long for a deeper connection with God and their husbands. One great aspect of this devotional is that it teaches and challenges wives to pray over their marriage! One of the greatest acts of love for our husband is to lift him up before the throne of God."
Ruth Schwenk / thebettermom.com

"This is not just another devotional to collect dust on your shelf. This sweet little book is a breath of fresh air inspired by the Lord Himself. I believe the author, Jennifer Smith, has had an intense face to face encounter with God. I believe He truly changed her heart and soul by reaching deep down and divinely touching and inspiring the darkest, most intimate parts of her very womanhood. She has been transformed and renewed and she shares her heart on how to love, honor and cherish God and our husbands with a humble honesty and sincerity. The result of her obeying God's calling on her life is the covenant marriage she knows today; the one He fully intended for her to have all along. I warn you, this is no easy read. Be prepared to be challenged. If you do the "work", you will be richly and deeply rewarded."
His Extraordinary Love Ministries

CONTENTS

A Letter To The Reader

Dear Wife,

It is such a wonderful blessing to share this devotional with you. God spoke to my heart encouraging, assisting, and inspiring me to provide a resource that would help draw you closer to Him and closer to your husband. I sincerely hope and pray this devotional is revolutionary in the two most important and intimate relationships in your life. I also want you to be encouraged knowing that there are many more wives journeying through this content, intentionally striving to be more holy as a child of God and as a wife; you are not alone in your struggles and you are not alone in your transformation of becoming the woman God created you to be. Knowing that you are rallying with wives all across the world to make positive changes in your heart and in your marriage should be empowering! If this devotional influences you and encourages you, please do not hesitate to share it with another wife. Thank you so much for taking the time to explore this devotional, for being a wife after God, and for investing in your marriage. May faith, hope, and love abound, and may peace fill your heart!

Love,
Jennifer Smith
Unveiled Wife

Dear Lord,

Thank You for this beautiful woman reading this right now. Thank You for giving her the opportunity to be a wife. May You bless her and her husband. May You fulfill their marriage in every way. Equip them with communication skills, inspire them to live intentionally, help them to cultivate intimacy, and allow them to experience the extraordinary. I pray her husband would see Your light radiating from her heart as she journeys through this devotional. May You radically transform their marriage so they would mirror Your love. I pray Your Holy Spirit would prepare this wife's heart for the material in this devotional. Soften her, Lord, so that she may gain understanding and wisdom. Give her courage to accept the challenges and to initiate them. I pray against the enemy, in Jesus' name. I pray against distractions that would try to steal her away from being able to complete this devotional. I implore You to send encouragements to her daily and to protect her and her marriage from any schemes or temptations the enemy attempts. Guard her heart and her mind in Christ Jesus. Reveal Yourself to her, Lord, in great and mighty ways, intimate ways, ways that are personal, so she comes to know You better. Thank You for her precious life. May You fill her with Your peace and help her grow in faith. Show her how to keep You in the center of her marriage as she becomes the wife you have called her to be.

In Jesus' name, AMEN!

INTRODUCTION

You are here because God pursued you. You are more valuable than treasured gold, silver, or gems. You are worthy to be loved and you are a wife! God has set aside a very special opportunity for husbands and wives to experience an intimate relationship with each other, which reflects the intimacy God desires to have with all of humanity! Your role as a wife is extraordinary because you have the opportunity to love, care for, and respect your husband with the unconditional love you receive from Christ.

Unfortunately, you live in a fallen world--your culture, environment, and family tree have influenced who you are today, and not all of the things you have learned along the way are beneficial. You can probably think about a few things right now that you know you need to work on. The more you humble yourself before God and ask Him to transform you, the better you become at fulfilling your purpose as a wife, which in turn leads to the fulfillment of a healthy, joyful, God-centered marriage. Of course, reaching the goal of a healthy, joyful, God-centered marriage will also require your husband to take action if he has not done so already. Your husband may be ahead of you in this area, he may be right alongside you, he may be ten steps behind you, or perhaps on a different path altogether. Wherever your husband is spiritually you need to trust God with him and continue to pray for him no matter what. Your husband needs you to do the same things you would want from him: to cheer him on, to set an example, to have faith, and to pursue him passionately.

As a Christian and as a wife, there is a responsibility to nurture both your relationship with God and your husband. Failure to passionately pursue these relationships will result in isolation. You may know that feeling all too well, but you can stand again and fight for what God has gifted to you. To do so you must take hold of your responsibilities and commit to working toward growth and oneness.

This devotional is designed to walk you through an intense journey of experiencing God, specifically tailored to one of your most important ministry roles-- being a wife! Here are some scriptures that support the purpose of this devotional:

Please Read

JAMES 4:8, HEBREWS 10:22, COLOSSIANS 2:2-3

These scriptures are foundational to the purpose of this devotional. God has called you to draw close to Him, to know the message of Christ, and to be encouraged. These things occur when you meditate on His Word.

This devotional has 30 chapters, so for the next 30 days I challenge you to commit to the following:

- Spending quality time with God daily through reading God's Word, praying, and journaling.
- Actively engaging and participating in all of the given challenges within each chapter.

You may or may not be familiar with spending time with God on a daily basis. Whether you are experienced with this or not, here are a few quick tips on how you can spend quality time with God:

You will need a Bible.

It is written in Hebrews 4:12 that God's Word is living and active. Just as you would carry a conversation with a close friend, God will converse with you through His Word. Keep in mind that reflecting on different Bible translations can provide more understanding of scripture. Feel free to explore different translations as you are going through the verses provided in this devotional.

You will be encouraged to journal.

Writing is one of the most comprehensive ways to learn because it forces you to slow down in your thinking process, allowing your hand a chance to translate your thought. It is also very beneficial in that you will have the opportunity to refer back to any archived entry and see your relationship growth with God along with any answered or unanswered prayers you may have written down. This devotional has space for you to journal within each chapter, but you may also use your own journal if you wish.

Sample Journal Entry

Here is a journal entry excerpt for you to use as a guideline if you do use a separate journal; however, there is freedom to customize your personal journal:

(Date) 11-24-10

(What God Is Teaching You) I need to stop worrying and give all of my cares to God. I need to keep praying everyday. I need to lean on God's understanding and not my own.

(Answer Questions From Devotional) My worry stems from fears or insecurities that I won't have enough to get by.

(Prayer) God, please help me not to worry about my kids or my job. Please give me confidence in the plans You have for me. I pray that You bless my husband and give him patience today. May Your will be done in my life, in Jesus' name Amen!

When you spend quality time with God, growth in your relationship with Him is inevitable. The amount of time you spend with God and the length of your journal entry is completely up to you, just be sure to pray, read scripture, and record what you experience. Remember, God wants to hear from you and He wants you to listen; the balance of both of these will result in great communication--the key to any thriving relationship.

Consistency is very crucial, both in your quality time with God and in participating in the challenges. Consistency reflects commitment and self-discipline. Some of the challenges will be more difficult than others; however, the result is a stronger relationship with God and with your husband. You must understand that this devotional is only as effective as you are willing to commit, and the devotion you exert, especially in your relationship with God, will overflow into your relationship with your husband.

Additionally, each chapter has a status update challenge. This is an incredible way for you to share your journey through the devotional with the Unveiled Wife Community as well as with other wives you may know. Participating in the social updates can be the inspiration other wives may need to put effort toward their relationship with God. All you need to do is copy the status update and send it out through social media being sure to tag @unveiledwife and #WifeAfterGod.

By committing to complete this 30 day devotional you will allow God to transform your life, your marriage, and you will inspire countless others who you will positively affect as you live out being a Wife After God!

*Sign below as a declaration to yourself and to God of the commitment you are making:

X _____

Invite a few other wives to grab a devotional and go through it at the same time. That way you will have some great discussion together over the material, you can keep each other accountable to the commitment you made, and learn how it is impacting each other's marriage!

Also, keep in mind that a version of this devotional is available as a group study! Visit WivesAfterGod.com for more details.

Encourage your husband in his walk with God with the husband companion version to this devotional titled Husband After God available at shop.unveiledwife.com.

GOD'S PURPOSE FOR YOUR MARRIAGE

GENESIS 1:27, 2 CORINTHIANS 5:20

God created you in His image. In His image! You were
made as a representation, to reflect God's goodness,
and to radiate His love. You were not thrown together
with scraps, nor were you stitched together with
leftovers. You were divinely designed by the Creator
of the universe, you were inspired by Him, and you
were made with purpose. Can you feel the weight of
this knowledge? Does it fill your heart with delight and
worthiness? If you value God, you must value what
He has created in His image, and you must value the
purpose of why He created...you.

You were fearfully and wonderfully made in His image.
You were made to represent Him. Knowing this should
change the way you view your life. No longer should
you be motivated by your own desires or pursuits,
rather you should be motivated by how you reflect Him.
Through your actions, your words, your appearance,

and all the different areas of your life.

Your husband was also fearfully and wonderfully made in God's image. Valuing your husband and valuing how God designed him and what God purposed him for is important to consider. His purpose as a husband adds to the fullness of the purpose of your marriage.

God made man and woman in His image. A husband and wife are complementary, and the fullness of both of their designs reflect the fullness of God's image. You and your husband, the two of you together as husband and wife, reflect the fullness of God's image.

Just as God created man and woman, God created marriage: the union of a man and woman, joining together to become one flesh. As these counterparts are joined together they mirror an incredible love story, God's love story. A marriage mirrors the intimate relationship between Jesus and His bride, the Church. Just as Jesus demonstrated selfless, sacrificial love, you can imitate that same love toward your husband and he can do the same for you.

Marriage is an opportunity to bring glory to God as you reflect His love story. God's purpose for your marriage is not only to allow you to be a living representation of His love toward mankind, but also to allow your marriage to teach you to be more like Him.

Dear Lord,

Thank You so much for creating me in Your image. Knowing that I was made in Your image minimizes the things I tend to be unsatisfied with or complain about. Please change my heart to understand the weight of what it means to be made in Your image. I pray that Your Holy Spirit would help me to reflect Your goodness and Your love. Thank You for my husband. Thank You for joining us together, giving us the opportunity to reflect Your love story. I pray that You would also help my husband understand why he was created in Your image and that our marriage has purpose. I believe as we operate knowing that our marriage can reflect Your testimony and bring You glory, we will have a stronger marriage and experience the extraordinary. May Your will be done in my marriage.

In Jesus' name, AMEN!

Challenge: Spend time talking with your husband about how the two of you reflect God's image and discuss the purpose of marriage.

Status Update: "@unveiledwife God's purpose for my marriage is to reveal His love to the world." #WifeAfterGod

Journal Questions:

Why is it important to know God's purpose for your marriage?

How does knowing your marriage has purpose change the way you look at your life and your marriage?

What is one thing you will do differently in your marriage knowing that you are reflecting God's love story?

MARRIAGE BY DESIGN

PSALM 139:13-18, EPHESIANS 5:21-33

God was intentional about the quality of your design. Think about the incredible detail He put into making your body. Now think about the creativeness in your mental capacity along with your emotions. God spent time developing every part of what makes you...you! God was intentional about the quality of your design and He was intentional about the quality of your husband's design.

God made male and female. Although both are made in His image, the details in their design are very different. It is important to embrace these differences and celebrate God's good design. There are many details that make men and women different from each other, but it is important to note the difference in needs when it comes to marriage. God inspired Paul to note these differences to help husbands and wives along their journey. Although a husband and a wife both need love and respect from each other, God designed men to have a deep need for respect and women to have an overwhelming desire to be loved.

Men get reenergized by respect. It gives them confidence and speaks to their soul, laying the foundation for them to lead and love well. Women are reenergized by love. When a woman is pursued romantically and loved unconditionally, she feels accepted and secure, which lays the foundation for her to serve as a helper and to fulfill God's commandment for her to submit to her husband. This was God's great design for marriage: that you would respect your husband through your words and actions and that he would love you unconditionally just as Christ loves the Church. By satisfying these needs in marriage you and your husband will experience a rich relationship abundant in generosity, kindness, faithfulness, and intimacy.

Marriage by God's design requires that you live out what He has called you to do regardless of whether your husband is doing his part or not. This is one of the greatest difficulties to overcome in marriage, especially if you have been hurt or offended by your husband. The source of motivation to fulfill your husband's needs regardless of his actions comes from your ability to trust God and your desire to obey His Word. This is where reflecting God's love story comes into focus. You will be reflecting the same unconditional, sacrificial love that Christ displayed for His bride of undeserved sinners. That type of love is transforming and redeeming.

Dear Lord,

Thank You for your incredible design. Thank You for all of the detail You put into creation, and thank You for Your design of marriage. I pray for wisdom, so I may fully understand the correlation of marriage and the Gospel. May You help me fulfill my husband's need for respect regardless of whether he deserves it or not. I desire to be a wife who reflects your unconditional love. I desire to be a wife who respects her husband. Take away the selfish parts of my heart that seeks to justify why I should or should not do something for my husband. Help me to love like You! I also pray that You would reveal these truths to my husband. Help him understand that it is important to fulfill my needs. I hope and pray that our marriage would grow as we mature, and as we are refined.

In Jesus' name, AMEN!

Challenge:
Take a moment to consider all the detail God thought about when He created you. Write down 5 things about yourself that are unique, then thank God for these details. Also, find time today to tell your husband one reason why you respect him.

Status Update:
"@unveiledwife God's design for marriage is for me to respect my husband and submit to him."
#WifeAfterGod

Journal Questions:
In what ways does your husband show you love?

What is one thing that makes it hard for you to respect your husband?

What are some ways you can show your husband respect?

THE NEED FOR COMPANIONSHIP

GENESIS 2:18-22, ECCLESIASTES 4:9-12

Companionship, fellowship, camaraderie. It is a need that exists at the core of every heart. God created man, and in doing so He created the gift of companionship. God created Adam, walked with him, talked with him, and invited Adam to join in an incredible relationship with Him. God entrusted Adam with the opportunity to name every amazing animal. Part of companionship in a relationship is establishing trust and being able to rely on another. Imagine the honor Adam must have felt when God asked him to join in and assist. God knew Adam's ability to fulfill such a task because they were companions. They knew each other, they spent time together, they stood side by side and endured life together. Even when there was conflict in their relationship, God protected Adam and sought reconciliation.

God desires companionship with you, as well. He wants to cultivate an intimate relationship with you, and He longs for you to join Him. He pursues you as a gentleman pursues a woman. He impresses you with creation, magnificent sunsets, brilliant flowers, and powerful seas. He woos you with poetic language, sweet aromas, and courts you with His Holy Spirit. Be still, look around you, see how the Lord is pursuing you!

How is He inviting you to join Him?

He is seeking companionship with you--an unending bond of intimate friendship. He is there beside you to be your rock, your refuge, your ally. He is there to share joy with you, to comfort you in times of hardship, and to help you weather every storm. There is nothing you can do to push Him away or to make Him not love you. However, to love God is a choice you must make because you have free will, which is the very thing that makes companionship so powerful...because you chose it.

Companionship emerged with the special relationship between God and man, yet God desired that man would have the opportunity to experience that same level of intimacy with a counterpart. That is when God put Adam to sleep and fashioned the most beautiful complement for him: woman. God intentionally created man and woman in His image, giving them the gift of companionship, a strong bond of friendship, camaraderie, and community, thus laying the foundations for marriage.

You were created for companionship. There was an extraordinary moment in your life when you stepped into a covenantal bond of companionship, choosing to love your husband, and declaring it with your vows. In that moment you became a wife. You said yes to standing side by side, to enjoying life together, enduring storms together, comforting one another, and making yourselves known to each other through intimate conversations and experiences. You said yes.

To have a thriving marriage you must protect your companionship with your husband. Make it a priority to pursue your husband, to invite him to join you, to commune with him and communicate with him. Trust in him, be confident in his abilities, rely on him, and rally with him. Be his friend and experience the marvelous gift of companionship.

Dear Lord,

*Thank You for pursuing me. Thank You for
caring about me and wanting companionship
with me. Please forgive me if I didn't
recognize all the times You were inviting
me to join You. Please open my eyes so that
I never miss out on those moments to share
with You. I pray that my relationship with
You continues to grow. I pray that you would
trust me and that I would trust You. I also
thank You for companionship in marriage.
Thank You for the bond that my husband and
I have, our friendship, and our intimacy. I
pray that my husband and I would cultivate
our companionship, that we would enjoy life
together, comfort each other, and stand by
each other to weather through every storm.
May You help me to trust in my husband
and be confident in his abilities. Please help
me to be intentional about investing in our
companionship and to be creative in pursuing
my husband daily.*

In Jesus' name, AMEN!

Challenge:
Spend time with your husband doing an activity that he would prefer to do.

Status Update:
"@unveiledwife I am going to pursue companionship with my husband." #WifeAfterGod

Journal Questions:
In what ways do you see God pursuing companionship with you?

Do you trust your husband to fulfill tasks in your marriage just like God allowed Adam to name the animals?

What is one thing you can do to build companionship with your husband?

DAY 4

YOUR SPOUSE IS A GIFT

GENESIS 2:21-25, PROVERBS 18:22

Bright white lights pushed back the darkness as a husband wrapped his arm around his wife, whispering to her, "I know we had agreed on a limit, but I feel God asking us to pay for one more person, is that okay?" Trusting in her husband and trusting in God, the wife said yes. They walked up to a man who had just pulled into the gas station. His tough appearance would keep most strangers at a distance, but this couple felt the Holy Spirit leading them to him.

The husband inquired, "Excuse me, sir, would you mind if we paid for your gas tonight?"

The man bowed his head in humbleness, tears streaming down his face. He had just spent his last bit of money at The Dollar Store buying Christmas gifts for his children. His mind had been racing at the thought of how he would make it home with no gas and no money, yet eager to bless his precious children. His head hung in disbelief that a random couple would show up to help him in a time of need.

The husband and wife were in awe of this man's
vulnerability and what he was sharing with them.
Their conversation lasted only 20 minutes. The couple
ministered to the man and prayed over him. In addition
to filling up the man's gas tank, the husband reached
into his wallet, shocked to find cash (something he
rarely ever carried), he generously handed all that he
had to the man, sharing with him that God wanted him
to have it. The man received the gift, thanked them,
and headed home to spend Christmas with his family.
Forever changed, forever blessed by the gift.

Adam was in awe of the breathtaking gift God had
given him--a spouse, his beautiful wife. Recognizing
her as his counterpart, Adam received his wife as a
gift from God, not because of anything she did, but
simply because he knew God and trusted God. Forever
changed, forever blessed by the gift.

Likewise, your husband is a gift from God. A
breathtaking, awe-inspiring gift--your counterpart,
your husband. Will you humbly receive your gift from
God because you trust God, receiving your gift with
thankfulness and joy? Or will you reject your gift from
God as if it is not good enough? Your attitude toward
your husband will reflect how you receive your gift.

You are also a gift! A precious and powerful gift--a
counterpart, a wife. It is important to see your husband

and yourself as gifts to each other everyday you have together, for that will influence how you treat each other.

The marriage relationship is also a magnificent gift in that you and your husband have the opportunity to bless others. Your marriage is a ministry where you and your husband can work together as a team to fulfill the needs of people around you, to show hospitality, to pray for people, to show compassion, to love by reflecting Christ's love as you mirror His image. Your marriage is a gift.

Dear Lord,

Thank You so much for the gift You have blessed me with, my husband and our marriage. Please forgive me for not always receiving this gift with thankfulness and joy. I pray that You would transform my heart and my perspective so that I may always recognize this powerful gift. I desire to have a deep appreciation for my husband that helps me treat him really good. May Your Holy Spirit remind me daily of this precious gift. I pray for my husband to understand that I am a gift, as well. Reveal to him this truth like You revealed it to me. Thank You for caring about us so much that You would give us the opportunity to experience marriage. May we live as a team to minister to others. May our hearts be sensitive to where You are calling us and to whom You are asking us to bless. May we be prepared to give as You ask of us, regardless of how big or small. I pray that others would see Your love story reflected through our love.

In Jesus' name, AMEN!

Challenge:
When you see your husband next, picture God handing him to you as a gift, and receive your gift by hugging your husband.

Status Update:
"@unveiledwife My husband is a gift from God."
#WifeAfterGod

Journal Questions:
What other gifts have you received from God?

How does your attitude toward your husband reflect how you perceive God's gift?

How can you and your husband be a gift to others?

TRANSFORMING LOVE

MATTHEW 27:27-54, HEBREWS 10:14, 1 PETER 2:24,

JOHN 3:16, JOHN 14:6, JOHN 15:13

Struggling to lift up His own weight, He staggered down a dirt path. Pain radiated throughout His body, His Spirit crushed by insult and mockery. Despite the excruciating affliction, He continued to walk, knowing that His destination would lead Him to even more suffering. Heavy, splintering wood pressed against His back, joining in with gravity to pull this man to the dusty ground. Anguish gripped His heart, yet He walked. Blood dripped from raw wounds, yet He carried on. There was no rescue plan. This man knew that He would experience death, but only after the shock of agony pierced His flesh. Still, He walked on, headed toward the place where He would breathe His last. His motivation was you.

Jesus Christ was sacrificed for you and for all mankind. He endured harsh treatment that led to death on the cross, providing people redemption from sin and the only way to be reconciled to God. He made that walk in humiliation regardless of whether or not anyone accepts Him as Lord and Savior. He didn't do it because you deserve it or because you earned it. There is only one way He could have endured that immense amount of pain: true, unconditional, selfless love.

Knowing that someone would go through so much for you regardless of how you respond, strips away any reason apart from love. The power of that kind of love is transforming. It transforms those who believe in it, drawing them closer to God, thus transforming their character to be more like His.

The power of that kind of love also transforms marriage. You have the opportunity to express the love of Christ toward your husband, regardless of if he deserves it or earns it. You can endure like Christ endured because you love unconditionally and sacrificially. In doing so your marriage will reflect God's love story, the story of reconciliation.

Dear Lord,

I appreciate You and all that You endured on the cross. Thank You for loving me unconditionally. I am so sorry that my sin caused You so much pain. If there is any sin in my life please reveal it to me so that I may repent. Draw me closer to You and transform my character to by like yours. May Your Holy Spirit remind me of Your sacrificial love daily so that I may strive to love my husband in the same way. Please take away my pride and anything that would keep me from loving my husband selflessly. Change my perspective so that I don't withhold love because I feel as if he doesn't deserve my love or hasn't earned it. I pray that I would be motivated to love my husband regardless of how he responds. I desire to have a marriage that mirrors Your love story so that You may be glorified. Thank You for the gift of marriage and the opportunity to love in such a great way.

In Jesus' name, Amen!

Challenge:
Christ endured so much because He loves you so much. Consider all that you have endured or are enduring currently in your marriage that shows your husband that you love him. Go the extra mile tonight to do something specific for your husband that shows him how much you love him.

Status Update:
"@unveiledwife Christ is my example for how to love others, especially how I should love my husband." #WifeAfterGod

Journal Questions:
What are three ways in which Jesus was a great example for how you should love your husband?

Where can you find the strength and motivation to love your husband especially when he doesn't deserve it?

What things tempt you to withhold your love from your husband?

How can you show your husband you love him unconditionally?

MINISTRY OF RECONCILIATION

ROMANS 5:18-19, 2 CORINTHIANS 5:17-20

When Adam and Eve sinned in the Garden of
Eden, they severed their intimate bond with God.
Although God never left them, there was conflict
in their relationship because of sin. God sought to
reconcile His relationship with man and did so, once
and for all, through His Son, Jesus Christ. Christ's
one act of sacrificial love, being the atonement for
sin, brought righteousness to all by the gift of grace,
allowing everyone the opportunity to have an intimate
relationship with God.

Reconciliation redeems relationships, restoring
harmony, peace, and agreement.

God has given you the ministry of reconciliation,
making you an ambassador to be at peace with others
and to appeal to others God's gift of amazing grace. You
have been given the ministry of reconciliation in your
marriage. This requires you to extend God's grace and

the message of the Gospel to your husband, mirroring Christ's love despite circumstance or situation.

You should walk in humility, forgiving your husband as God has forgiven you, restoring harmony, peace, and agreement in your marriage. Remember, Christ did not wait for an apology from anyone before surrendering Himself in humility to make things right. Instead, He initiated by acting first. As a wife, you have a remarkable opportunity to experience the awesome power of reconciliation as you seek to restore your relationship with your husband at any sign of discord or sin. This is not an easy thing to do. Your pride will tempt you to withhold, your intellect will try to justify what is fair, and your heart will attempt to manipulate your motives. However, if you fight your flesh as Jesus did, for the sake of reconciliation, your marriage will thrive with true intimacy.

Dear Lord,

Thank You for initiating in our relationship. You pursue me with love and compassion. Thank You for reconciling my relationship with You, so that we may experience intimacy. I love You, Lord! I pray that I would gain a deeper understanding of how You reconciled our relationship through Christ. Fill me with Your wisdom and show me how to love like You. I pray that I can be a wife who seeks to reconcile with my husband. Help me to initiate reconciliation in my marriage. Remove any pride and humble me, Lord. Holy Spirit, convict my heart and give me the strength to fight against my flesh as I try to respond to my husband with the intentions of making peace. I pray that my husband would also seek to reconcile with me. Help us as we experience the ministry of reconciliation together.

In Jesus' name, Amen!

Challenge:
Initiate reconciliation by forgiving your husband, whether with a past offense or with the next disagreement or sin. Also, acknowledge the gift of grace God has offered to you and receive it whole-heartedly.

Status Update: "@unveiledwife I have the ministry of reconciliation through Christ and I can initiate true intimacy by reconciling with my husband." #WifeAfterGod

Journal Questions:
How did God reconcile the world to Himself?

What usually keeps you from mending your relationship with your husband after an argument or offense?

How can you participate in the ministry of reconciliation in your marriage?

MARRIAGE IS TO MAKE YOU HOLY

COLOSSIANS 2:6-7, ROMANS 6:22, GALATIANS 5:17

Sanctification means to be set apart. When a person accepts Jesus as Lord and Savior, they are set apart from the rest of the world; they become a Christian--one who follows Christ. In this sense, sanctification occurs when we are saved, in that by divine grace sins are covered and forgiveness is granted. However, sanctification can also be defined as a process of transformation to become more like Christ. As a Christian, you are set apart to be made holy. So, sanctification is an event and a process of transformation.

Even though you are saved through grace, you have habits and characteristics from your old self that need to be transformed and made new by God. This produces an inner struggle of sin and holiness between your flesh and spirit. Although this conflict can be difficult to experience, the more you trust in God's ways, and practice godliness, the more your character will be transformed.

Did you know that gold goes through a refining process? Fire is used to heat gold to extreme temperatures in order to remove any impurities; what is left is pure gold. Likewise, you will go through fire; you will experience hardships, trials, and tests. You will face things that will cause inner conflict as you learn to let go of your old ways, while embracing God's ways. God's Spirit was sent to comfort you, to help you, and to sanctify you. As the Holy Spirit leads you through change, you will become refined, pure, holy.

In Ephesians 5:21-33 Paul mentions the profound correlation between Christ's relationship with the Church and the relationship between a husband and wife. The two love stories mirror each other in great ways--one of which is sanctification. It is an event AND a process of transformation. On your wedding day you entered into a covenant with your husband where you were set apart exclusively for him, a memorable event that will forever be imprinted in your mind. And yet, marriage is also a process of transformation, learning how to adjust from your old ways of being single, to thinking of another, namely, your husband. You experience hardships, trials, and tests together as companions--as husband and wife. You will also face conflict in marriage with the realization that sin surfaces in such an intimate relationship. Marriage is not just to make you happy by fulfilling all of your needs. Marriage is to make you holy by refining you through a process of transformation.

You are a wife, committed to your husband. No longer operating in selfishness, you now seek to serve, respect, and love your husband. Your marriage will give you ample opportunity to grow and mature. The changes you will experience through the different seasons of marriage will lead you to refinement if you intentionally choose to accept marriage as a way for God to transform you. The choice to embrace God's ways will always be up to you and it will always begin by submitting yourself to Him.

Dear Lord,

You are marvelous. You carefully and intentionally designed marriage to represent so much of Your love story. Thank You for opening my eyes to the correlations. May Your Holy Spirit write Your truth on my heart so that I never forget it. Thank You for sanctifying me through Jesus Christ. Thank You for making me holy. I submit my life to You and I submit my marriage to You. May Your will be done, Lord! I lift up my husband to You. I ask that You would teach him Your ways and that he too would submit his life to You. I pray that he would lead me as Christ leads the Church. Please show me how I can bless my husband today. When we go through difficult times, trials, and tests please watch over us and help us to navigate through them. I pray that You guide my husband and I to choose Your ways. As I face inner struggles of sin please help me to overcome my flesh and choose to live by the Spirit. I choose You, Lord.

In Jesus' name, AMEN!

Challenge:
Let your wedding ring, a precious metal that endured refining fire and was crafted into a perfect unending circle, serve as a reminder to you to pray for your marriage. (If you do not have a wedding ring, let your ring finger be your reminder to pray for your marriage.)

Status Update:
"@unveiledwife Marriage is not just to make me happy, but to make me holy." #WifeAfterGod

Journal Questions:
In what ways are you sanctified or "set apart" as a wife?

What transformations are you currently experiencing as a Christian or as a wife?

How can you respond to your husband differently knowing that the trials you face together have the potential to produce transformation in your marriage?

DAY 8

Confident Worthiness

PROVERBS 31:10, PSALM 139:13-18, PSALM 23

You are worthy. Regardless of whether you have insecurities, sin, or fear...you are worthy. You were created with intention and you matter.

God, the Creator of the universe, your Maker, formed you in your mother's womb with thoughtfulness, precision, and purpose. He knows you better than anyone could ever know you. God passionately and undoubtedly loves you. He longs for you to grasp the depths of His great love for you. He desires you to be confident in knowing that He finds you worthy. He wants to be enough for you. God yearns to be your everything.

God is the only one who has the power to be your everything. His compassion has the capability to fill your heart with warmth more calming than sun rays falling upon your cheek. His peace transcends every layer of your being and eclipses the most anxious of thoughts. His grace is extended freely, covering your sin nature with a robe woven for royalty. His resources are unlimited. His strength is beyond comprehension. His economy is stable. His provision is perfect. He pursues you with creativity. He speaks softly to you...so softly that only your heart would know it was Him.

He comforts you with light touches, the way the wind drifts across your skin. He leads you to green pastures and quiet waters where you can have a moment to be still and to rest in Him. He initiates intimacy with you, drawing you to converse with Him, to ask of Him, and to make yourself known to Him. God is the only one who can meet your every desire, exceed your every expectation, and fulfill your life completely...because He loves you and believes you are worth it.

Will you be honest with yourself and evaluate your life to see if you allow God to be your everything? Do you seek your worthiness in God alone? Do you find Him worthy of your trust?

There are many other things in this world that you can put your trust in and many different ways you can seek to find affirmation of your worthiness, but nothing will be able to fulfill you like God can. For example, you have probably sought worthiness from your husband. But, there will be times that he lets you down, times he will not meet your expectations, times he will break your trust, times where he won't think to comfort you or chooses not to because of pride. There are even times he will neglect to pursue you and times that he won't think you are worthy. Why? Because he is only human, prone to sin and selfishness. This will lead you to thoughts of disappointment spurring a belief in your heart that you are not worthy. When a heart is downcast in such a way it hinders a person from being able to live joyfully and serve compassionately. When a wife feels unworthy it halts the marriage from experiencing extraordinary.

However, if you seek your worthiness in God, being fulfilled completely by Him, then you are able to unconditionally love your husband regardless of whether he fulfills you or fails you, thus mirroring God's love story. You are worthy. Your husband is worthy. Your marriage is worth fighting for, and worth submitting to God. Seeking your worthiness in God means that you confidently trust in Him and accept His Word as truth. Confident worthiness is a result of allowing God to be your everything.

Dear Lord,

Thank You for finding me worthy. I am sorry that I do not always see my worthiness. Sometimes I get so insecure and I look to my husband to fulfill me or comfort me. This fear-based love keeps me from enjoying my marriage and it leaves me feeling unworthy. I trust You and I trust that You do find me worthy. Thank You for all the ways You show me I am worthy. Please help me have confidence! I pray that I would seek You daily and allow You to be my everything! May my marriage be blessed as I submit my role as a wife to You, asking that You transform me into the woman You created me to be. I lift up my husband, praying that he too would find his worthiness in You. You are worthy God of my heart and my faith.

In Jesus' name, AMEN!

Challenge:
Take a walk with your husband or watch a sunset together and talk about all the ways that God may be showing you your worthiness. You can also talk about how God may be asking you to trust Him with a specific area of your marriage.

Status Update:
"@unveiledwife I find my worthiness in God alone and only He can fulfill me." #WifeAfterGod

Journal Questions:
What evidence convinces you of your worthiness?

Where is the first place you usually go when you desire to feel worthy?

How can trusting in God fulfill your need to feel worthy?

THE GOOD WIFE

A woman sat quietly with her hands clasped together in her lap. Eyes swollen, tears rolling down her cheeks, pleading with God for one request. Her heart ached. Her thoughts swirled. Humbled by amazing grace she prayed, for over 30 years she prayed, the same one request,

"Lord, I pray that my husband accepts Christ as Lord and Savior. I pray he knows You. Lord, save him."

Her marriage encountered many different seasons and many difficult ones. Despite years of hardship, feelings of inadequacy, loneliness, and severed intimacy, she stood by her husband. Her husband resisted God and he refused to join his wife at church. Yet, this wife continued to love and respect her husband. She was led by faith and chose to mirror God's love story by being like Christ in her home. Her choice to love unconditionally was met with daily obstacles, yet she remained strong and loved well. Her motivation was a conviction that salvation for her husband was the most important thing.

A week before her husband passed away, he had accepted Christ into his life. This woman recounts the last days she spent with him,

"He was a different man, loving, and peaceful."

God answered her longing, her cry, her prayer. She loved her husband so much and considered it worth it--every prayer, every tear, and every sacrifice. She felt as if it was her purpose as his wife to stand by him, to stand firm in faith, and to pray.

This woman was intentional about being a good wife. Regardless of her husband's response toward her, regardless of his behavior, regardless of his thoughts, she loved him unconditionally. She brought him good and not harm all the days of his life. She endured because she believed he and his salvation were worth fighting for.

Being a good wife begins with your relationship with God. As you walk with God, the Holy Spirit will transform your heart and your character, teaching you what is right. With your eyes focused on God you become a light to others through your words and through your actions. God is your source of energy, your source of hope, and your source of strength to endure every season of life. The closer you draw to God, the more your faith will grow, your joy will abound, and your desire to be a good wife will inevitably increase.

You are called to be a good wife. Do not grow weary in doing good, for in time your marriage will reap a harvest that will produce extraordinary. For the good wife mentioned above, the harvest was salvation for her husband. It may be the same for you or it may be experiencing more intimacy or more adventures or more laughter or more comfort. You must have faith! Trust in God, pray continually, and lean on Him to be your strength. Hang in there, friend, you can do this. Bring good to your husband all the days of his life. He is worth it. Regardless of his sin, he is worth it.

Dear Lord,

Thank You for my husband. Thank You for showing me that my husband is also worthy. Despite his sin, You find him worthy. Please help me to see him worthy like You do. Help me to be a good wife to him all the days of his life. May Your Holy Spirit teach me what is right and inspire me to pray for my husband as he needs. I pray my faithfulness increases! Remind me daily to lift him up to You. May You be my strength and may I lean on You daily so that I never grow weary in doing good for him. I pray that You would use me to be a beacon of light, Christ's light, to shine in our home.

In Jesus' name, AMEN!

Challenge:
Find one specific way to put your husband's needs above your own today.

Status Update:
"@unveiledwife I am a wife who finds her strength in God to do good." #WifeAfterGod

Journal Questions:
What motivates you to treat your husband good?

What keeps you from treating your husband good?

Do you believe your husband's salvation is the most important thing?

PERFECT POSTURE

PSALMS 95:6, 2 SAMUEL 6:14-15,

MATTHEW 26:6-13, 1 PETER 2:13-25

"Posture"--the way in which you pose your body. This includes many different positions, such as standing, sitting, and kneeling. Your body can also contort in many different ways to express the other kind of posture...your attitude! These expressions include eye rolling, hands on the hips, and arms crossed poses, just to name a few. Attitude is the posture of your heart. Your attitude is expressed through your words, tone of voice, and physically through your body language. Variations are ample and your motives for expressing such postures are countless.

Worship postures reflect reverence and respect to God. The Bible is filled with scriptures that describe different positions of worshipping and praising God, including kneeling before the Lord and lifting hands up high. This type of body language reveals humility and honor to

God. There are also stories of people mentioned in the Bible whose actions revealed the posture of their heart, like David dancing before the Lord or the woman in Bethany who anointed Jesus with precious oil. David's action revealed the joy he was experiencing in his heart, while the woman in Bethany revealed selflessness and reverence.

Another great illustration from the Bible is the story of Jesus, who lived a Holy life prior to being arrested and sentenced to death by crucifixion. Jesus Christ, perfect in every way, became a scapegoat, enduring the consequences of every sin ever committed. Through His actions He exemplified perfect posture. He was ridiculed and mocked, yet He kept quiet. He carried the weight of the wooden cross on His back and the sins of the world on His shoulders, yet He did not complain. His arms spread out with vulnerability, yet He did not try to hang onto His life. The posture of His heart revealed humility, compassion, selflessness, patience, and unconditional love.

How is your posture? Have you ever thought about the impact it makes when you are communicating with others?

When you worship and praise God you can honor Him with your body. Just as a loyal servant would bow before a king, you can show reverence for God, the King of kings! This does not have to take place only during a church service. Your praise and worship is a lifestyle. It is a culmination of how and why you acknowledge God on a daily basis, and it requires sacrifice and humility.

As a wife you have a tremendous opportunity to mimic Christ's perfect posture toward your husband. Your actions that occur as a result of your attitude, play a huge role in your daily communications with your husband. You can choose to operate out of selfishness and disrespect by justifying your body language, or you can choose to live in obedience to Christ with self-control as you contort your posture to reflect humility, compassion, selflessness, patience, and unconditional love. By expressing the latter you will win your husband over with true love, fill your home with peace, and provide an atmosphere for intimacy to flourish. This choice that confronts you exists with every new day.

Dear Lord,

I am in awe of the posture Jesus carried while enduring so much agony. Despite the emotional, mental, and physical pain that He experienced, He continued knowing the good that would come from His response to it all. Salvation. Thank You, Jesus, for Your sacrifice! I desire to have perfect posture like You. Please help me to control my attitudes, as well as my body language. Whether I am praising You, God, or communicating with my husband, I pray that I would be aware of the condition of my heart. I pray that I would have Your characteristics, including humility, compassion, selflessness, patience, and unconditional love. Thank You for showing me how important it is to be aware of my posture. Please remind me everyday to choose righteousness over selfishness. As I change this area of my life with Your help, I pray that my husband sees and appreciates the effort, and may it inspire him to be intentional with his posture. May our marriage experience a revolution in how we communicate and the attitudes we carry.

In Jesus' name, AMEN!

Challenge:
Be aware of how your attitude is expressed through your body language. During your next encounter with your husband, check the position of your posture and if it is not reflecting Christ, take a quick moment to pray and then attempt to make adjustments. Spend time journaling about being more aware of your postures.

Status Update:
"@unveiledwife Attitude is the posture of the heart."
#WifeAfterGod

Journal Questions:
What are examples of positive and negative postures you have expressed toward your husband?

What kinds of things affect your attitude?

How can reflecting Christ's posture benefit your marriage?

PURE JOY

DEUTERONOMY 31:8, ROMANS 12:1-2, HEBREWS 12:1-3

Piles of clothes sat scattered across the bedroom floor along with sprinkles of children's toys. Maneuvering around the small spaces of clarity, a woman carried her three month old from a makeshift changing table to her bed. Lying down next to her precious child, she gazed intently at the beauty of her baby. Tears swelled in the corners of her eyes. As much as she longed to enjoy these treasured moments, anxiety crushed her spirit, stealing from her the time she would never be able to relive again. She had been struggling with anxiety for weeks, and no amount of assurance from her husband could logically explain what plagued her, leading to a belief that death was looming. Fear seized her heart while intense thoughts of disease manifested into physical symptoms. Tear after tear followed the same path down her cheek as she told God,

"I can't take this anymore, I don't know what to do."

Later that day her phone buzzed with a short text from a friend. It read, "Go check your doorstep." With her hands full, taking care of the baby, her husband ran downstairs to grab a small box that was left behind along with an even smaller envelope. He handed his wife the gift, hoping it would spark joy in her heart. Eager to open up the card, she read sweet words of encouragement:

I wanted to let you know I am praying for you. I came across this verse that I thought was fitting for you as you struggle with anxiety and health fears.

"It's The Lord who goes before you. He will be with you; He will not leave you or forsake you. Do not fear or be dismayed." (Deuteronomy 31:8)

I hope that verse will bring you the comfort and peace it has brought me. The Lord alone brings the soul ultimate comfort; however, I thought a cupcake might help too! Love, your friend!

The sides of her lips began to curl up as peace and gratefulness flooded her heart. The delicious aroma of buttercream frosting came bursting out of the small Tupperware box that came with the card. Her friend was another wife she met through the marriage Bible study at church. This wasn't the first time this wife extravagantly loved her, and it wouldn't be the last. She was anointed with the gift of hospitality--she was excited about celebrating life and bringing joy to others, creatively gifting treasures of food or kind words. Her random act of kindness did not cure the woman's anxiety, but it reminded her to lean on God. It encouraged her spirit, and it gave her strength to endure another day.

It is amazing knowing that people have the capacity to have an impact on the lives of others in such incredible ways. The friend in the story not only dropped off cupcakes, but she invited her friend to enjoy life with her. They went on walks together, they talked, they encouraged one another, and they served one another through their friendship. Being able to experience love like that requires sacrifice. The sacrifice of time, money, and energy. That kind of sacrifice screams, "You're worth it!" When people believe that others are worth it, extraordinary things happen.

Over a period of a year and a half the woman with the baby saw how her friend blessed her and others. She admired her friend deeply. One day she asked her friend, "What motivates you to love others so well?"

She responded, "God loves us! We are special to Him and He celebrates us. We are so valuable to Him. We are priceless. If we have God in our hearts we need to see and love others as He does, which means celebrating them and honoring them and making them feel valued and one of a kind!"
She never said anything about a sacrifice because she considered it pure joy, just as Jesus did when He was

sacrificed. Yet, her actions required sacrifice. It was a choice she made when she took the time to write the note of encouragement and spent money on ingredients to bake the cupcakes. Her motivation was to give others the opportunity to experience Christ's love--His extraordinary love.

You are called to be a living sacrifice. The downfall with a living sacrifice is that it has the ability to get up and walk off of the altar. Walking off the altar happens when you selfishly focus inward, which is the message of the world, the message we are not supposed to conform to. The story illustrated above is to show you what happens when you exude obedience by staying on the altar. You become the hands and feet of Jesus, loving others and fulfilling their needs while providing them the chance to experience extraordinary.

You can be Jesus' hands and feet by loving people just as God loves them. Of course, it will require you to sacrifice your time, your money, and your energy. However, when you serve God, it doesn't feel like a sacrifice, it feels like joy--pure joy. You can share that joy in your marriage as you serve your husband or in your friendships when you serve other wives. That kind of love screams, "You're worth it!" When people believe that others are worth it, extraordinary things happen.

Dear Lord,

Thank You for today. Thank You for all the blessings and the encouragements You have given to me. Thank You for using others to lavish me with Your love. I pray that You would use me in such great ways. I pray that I can be Jesus' hands and feet, serving others regardless of what sacrifices I have to make to do so. Please open my eyes to who You want me to bless. Show me how I can serve my husband and encourage him with random acts of kindness. Holy Spirit, remove selfishness from my heart so that I never walk off the altar! I want to be a living sacrifice! Help me not to conform to this world, but rather be a wife who is overflowing with joy, thoughtfulness, and incredible faith.

In Jesus' name, AMEN!

Challenge:
Take time to bless another wife today through a random act of kindness. Also, find one way to bless your husband!

Status Update:
"@unveiledwife I consider it pure joy to bless my husband and I am motivated by God's great love for me." #WifeAfterGod

Questions:
Describe a time when someone blessed you that really impacted your life?

What does it mean to you to be a living sacrifice?

Do you have any fears about being a living sacrifice?

THE ARMOR OF GOD

EPHESIANS 5:33, EPHESIANS 6:1-4,

EPHESIANS 6:10-18

The end of Ephesians 5 and the beginning of Ephesians 6 briefly mention the family unit. These scriptures lay out how husbands and wives should treat each other, as well as how parents and their children should treat each other. Your family is important to God, which is why He talks to you about it through His Word. God has incredible wisdom and insight that will benefit your family in great ways.

For example, strategically placed at the end of Ephesians 6 is a section of scripture detailing the Armor of God, explaining why you should put it on and how you can use it to protect you and your family. Just as a knight would equip himself with armor before battle, God asks you to equip yourself with His armor. God's wisdom exposes the reality of spiritual warfare, revealing to you the power you have to stand against evil forces. It is no coincidence that this part of scripture is expressed so closely to the brief mention of family relationships. God was intentional about its placement, knowing that our most intimate relationships would be a continuous target for the enemy's attacks. It is imperative that you heed God's wisdom for the sake of your loved ones. Take some time to examine each piece of the armor and how it will benefit your marriage, which in turn will bless your whole family.

Belt of Truth - First and foremost, you must believe God's truth--His Holy Word. When you are feeling attacked, offended, wounded, or overwhelmed, God's truth is the only comfort that will bring you healing and peace. You need to have a firm foundation in your heart of what God says about you. When hard times press, let His truthfulness keep you stable. The other part of this piece of armor is being a woman of your word. Truthfulness is having sincerity in your actions and your character. Truth is doing what you say you will do and being honest with your words. If you tell your husband you will fulfill a need of his at a certain time, you must follow through with your promise. By doing so, you build a reputation of truthfulness and trust with your husband. Truth in marriage creates a safe place for intimacy to increase.

Breastplate of Righteousness – The only true way to attain righteousness is to abide in Christ. As you submit to Christ in obedience, your character will be transformed to reflect His. The motivation to strive toward living a moral life comes from deep within your heart as your relationship with God develops. The breastplate protects the heart of a knight. Likewise, you can protect your heart from the destruction and havoc of sin by choosing to live according to God's ways. This is a daily choice you make when confronted with all kinds of decisions. By choosing righteousness you are saying yes to love, joy, peace, patience, kindness, goodness, faithfulness, gentleness, and self-control. Such a beautiful array of fruitfulness will enable your marriage to thrive.

Gospel of Peace   The good news of God's love story comes with the power of transcending peace. Only He can truly fill your heart with peace no matter how difficult of a situation you are facing. If you ever feel the weight of anxiety, depression, anger, fear, being overwhelmed, insecurity, unworthiness, or any other oppression that seizes your ability to function aptly, you must lean on Him to receive the power of His peace. There is nothing you can do to set yourself free and there is nothing your husband can do to make the oppression go away. Only God's peace can bring you healing and only He can set you free. So when the pressure builds and the enemy advances, be prepared to rely on God for peace. Having the readiness of peace also means that you pursue harmony no matter where you are and no matter what your circumstances are. Peace is especially vital to pursue in marriage. When you seek to be a peacemaker, selfishness diminishes, while love flourishes.

Shield of Faith – Faith is trusting in God, believing that His plans are best. In faith you believe that God's plan for you and your husband is better than anything you can ever imagine, because you know God's love for you both is great. Faith is also having confidence in things hoped for. If you hope to experience passionate intimacy with your husband, you must be confident in his ability to love you. If you hope to see your husband lead your family as a God-fearing man, you need to have confidence that he is capable of being that leader. If you hope to experience an awesome marriage with your husband, you should use your shield of faith to block any negativity from others, words that have the potential to put doubt in your heart. This will help you remain loyal to your husband and faithful to the hope you had when you first married him. Faith and hope feed your soul passion and purpose, which are elements needed to enjoy life.

Helmet of Salvation – Salvation is defined as deliverance from sin and preservation from destruction. Just as God extended grace to you, be diligent in extending grace to your husband for his sin, faults, and failures. Deliver your husband from weakness through forgiving him, praying for him, and giving him the opportunity to change. Be mindful that neither you, nor your husband are perfect, both of you are in need of daily grace. Preserve your marriage from destruction by investing in your marriage through gaining knowledge. Seek marriage resources that will enlighten your perspectives, inspire your passion, and challenge you to be transformed into the wife God desires you to be.

Sword of The Spirit - One of your most powerful weapons of defense will always be the Word of God. The Sword of the Spirit is the powerful Word of God, which is living and active, sharper than any double-edged sword. With God's Word you can learn how to live as He has called you to, you can learn about His truths, you can learn about His love story, and you can learn about how to invest in your love story. The Bible has power in it! Read it, memorize it, meditate on it, and lean on it for comfort and understanding. By actively utilizing the Bible, your faith will grow, your heart will be transformed, and your marriage will be blessed as you blossom into a beautiful, God-fearing wife.

Along with all of the different pieces of armor, you are also encouraged to pray. Faith enables you to pray; to communicate with your God, your Commander, your King. Through prayer you can give thanks and you can implore protection over your family. Prayer is a powerful way to keep your life, your marriage, and your family focused on God.

Ephesians 6:11 is a call to action. God is calling you to put on the armor, and not just pieces of it... the full armor of God! Perhaps you should make it part of your daily routine, dressing yourself spiritually to prepare you for the battles of the day. Your marriage and your family depend on you!

Dear Lord,

Thank You for sharing wisdom on how to defend and protect my family. I commit to putting on Your armor everyday! Please help me to be intentional in all of these specific areas of my life. I believe that as I use Your armor I will draw closer to You, while standing firm against the enemy! I pray that the enemy is halted in his plans to take my family. May You send angels to surround my home and to guard my marriage. Strengthen me, Lord, and give me the courage to stand firm in faithfulness and defend my faith, my marriage, and my family.

In Jesus' name, AMEN!

Challenge:
Memorize all the different pieces of the armor of God!

Status Update:
"@unveiledwife I am putting on the full armor of God for my marriage." #WifeAfterGod

Questions:
Why is it important for you to put on the full armor of God?

What could some of the "flaming arrows of the evil one" look like in your marriage?

What are three ways your marriage will benefit from wearing the armor of God?

COATED IN PRIDE

PROVERBS 8:13, PROVERBS 11:2, PROVERBS 13:10,

PROVERBS 16:18, MATTHEW 5:5

Pacing back and forth across the bedroom, his heart beat heavily inside his chest, feeling as if he was going to explode. He had just encountered an argument with his wife. What started out as a small disagreement quickly escalated like a science experiment gone wrong. Both of their hearts were coated in pride and neither would surrender. At the peak of their conflict, the wife stormed out of the bedroom and slammed the door. Her intentions were to halt the escalation and return when emotions subsided; however, the pride that darkened her heart also knew turning away and shutting the door would offend her husband all the more. With the distance between them growing, anger fueled their pride. Neither of them wanted to surrender, neither of them would forsake the argument for the sake of the other, and their focus was not love. Pride is an inflated opinion of oneself, a breeding ground for self-deception. Pride will convince you that your opinions, your actions, and your ways can all be justified as right. Acting on pride is dangerous because its goal is self preservation, not love. Pride is also dangerous because it keeps you from experiencing intimacy in your relationships. Pride speaks lies like, "I have the all the answers," or "I don't need you," or "I can do it on my own," or "My way is the right way." These postures of the heart make it impossible to experience intimacy with others. Rather, it has a polarizing effect, pushing people away.

Did you know that God hates pride? God hates pride because it will deceive you into believing that you don't need Him. Pride keeps you from being humble, it keeps you from admitting when you have sinned, it keeps you from praying, and it keeps you from leaning on God's truth. A heart full of pride is unteachable; therefore, the process of transformation is hindered. Pride quenches the Holy Spirit, severing your union with God. If you want an intimate relationship with God, you must let go of your pride.

Pride can also be destructive to your marriage. Many wives have lived in the same shoes as the wife mentioned above, slamming the door on her husband. Can you relate? Have you ever turned your back to your husband in frustration? Have you ever slammed a door on him? Have you ever yelled disrespectfully to fight for your way?
Pride is not motivated by love, it will keep you from

surrendering, it will keep you from apologizing, and it will keep you from forgiving. Pride gives birth to bitterness and resentment. Without reconciliation, a husband and wife who are one flesh are wounded fatally. Pride will cause you to fall, it will lead to ruin, and it will build giant walls made to suffocate intimacy in marriage. If you want a thriving relationship with your husband, you must let go of your pride.

Letting go of your pride is like removing your coat and hanging it up. You may take time to adjust to the climate, but your steps will be more intentional with the realization that you are vulnerable, exposed to other elements. However, God will cover you with a robe designated for royalty, for He blesses the humble. It will be as if you are trading rags for riches. You will be sensitive to His direction, you will yield to His ways, you will be aware of other's around you, and you will be love-focused. Letting go of your pride allows you to adopt God's perspective of your husband, your marriage, and your circumstances. Seeing things from His point of view and embracing His ways will give you greater understanding and help you respond to it all without sin.

Dear Lord,

Pride is so deceiving. There are many times that I don't even recognize its presence, disguised behind my own justifications. I pray that I would be aware of pride in my heart. I repent of having pride and I ask that You would remove it from me. Humble me Lord, for I desire to experience intimacy with You and with my husband. I need You, Lord! I cannot live without You and my heart knows this very well. I pray that I would never justify sin, that I will always initiate reconciliation, and that I would never respond toward my husband in prideful ways. Protect me from letting pride into my heart. Help me to extinguish it as soon as it appears. Thank You for encouraging me in this area of my life. I pray that everyday I can remain humble, intentional in my actions, and love-focused.

In Jesus' name, AMEN!

Challenge:
If you have been prideful about something specific in your marriage, let it go and see what happens!

Status Update:
"@unveiledwife I am letting go of my pride so that intimacy in my marriage can thrive." #WifeAfterGod

Questions:
Have you experienced pride in your heart and then experience a fall in your relationship with your husband because of it?

What is one thing you have been very prideful about recently and what do you feel God is calling you to do about it?

How does aligning your heart with God's heart help you to respond to situations without being prideful?

FORGIVENESS

Matthew 6:14-15, Matthew 18:21-22, Romans 5:1-5,

Colossians 3:12-14, 1 John 1:9

Fury raged within her heart as she drove down the road toward home. Her hands burned as she gripped the steering wheel--a result of the tension that was building. Her husband sat next to her, guilt-ridden, and ashamed of his weakness and sin. It was not the first time that he admitted his struggle with pornography. He knew it was wrong, he understood the weight of his sin, yet he gave into a fleeting illusion of satisfaction, again.

She was done crying over the pain that emerged from his infliction; anger was consuming her heart like a plague. Her mind was clouded with images he must have seen, only able to reason that his motivation was because she's not good enough. Insecurity and fear threatened her heart and their marriage.

Longing to be set free from his addiction, the man

gathered all the courage he had in him to be honest with his wife. He felt God's conviction, unable to escape the truth that he betrayed his wife. She said nothing in response, but her body language revealed how she felt. The ride home grew colder as the distance between them seemed to expand. Although the intensity of hurt filled her heart, the situation was familiar. In fact, they shared many conversations regarding this particular sin and how it affects their relationship and the potential it had to sever their marriage completely. She has cried, yelled, reasoned, and more, on many different occasions. Yet, he failed her again.

Amidst her pain, God spoke to her heart, "Forgive him."

Wrestling to be obedient, she whispers back, "I can't." God responded, "Yes you can, I will help you."

Distress grieved her as tears began to roll down her face. She asked God, "What about the pain? He hurt me so badly. I can't look at him the same."

God answered, "I will heal you and I will give you eyes to see as I see. Forgive him, just as I forgive you."

The wife pulled into the driveway, her husband sat quietly completely wrecked by what he had caused. In her brokenness she looked into his eyes and said, "I forgive you." Reaching her arms around him they fell into each other, reminded of how vulnerable their marriage is and the responsibility they had to protect it. The grace she extended in that moment and her love for her husband covered his sin like water being thrown on a fire, paving the way for reconciliation.

Marriage is vulnerable because it is an intimate union between two sinners. You and your husband have personal struggles and sins that impact your marriage in huge ways. There will be times when you will fail your husband and times when he will fail you. Without forgiveness, ruin in your relationship is inevitable.

There are many different issues that can cause conflict in marriage, pornography is just one example. Other sources of contention that may arise in marriage are finances, manipulation, lying, family, perspectives, preferences, pride...the list goes on. However, if you are willing to extend forgiveness--true forgiveness--the power of reconciliation can transform these conflicts into milestones of growth. Christ encourages you to continue to forgive just like He continues to forgive you. Do you grasp the depth of this incredible gift of being able to forgive? As you choose to forgive your husband, you experience the power and authority of Jesus! And you are able to forgive because God's love has been poured into your heart through the Holy Spirit!

It is important to highlight the other side of this argument, the power of apology. Humility is required to apologize because you are surrendering, you are admitting a wrongdoing, you are acknowledging the pain you caused another, you are confessing to sin. A sincere apology should be able to stand alone, regardless of whether your husband chooses to forgive you or not. If your apology is contingent on how he responds, then you are not truly surrendering.

Apology and forgiveness are vital signs of a healthy marriage. Do your part to keep your marriage strong through your willingness of practicing these necessary elements that lead to reconciliation.

Dear Lord,

I understand the responsibility I have to do my part in my relationship with You and my relationship with my husband. Please continue to reveal to me what my part is. I am so sorry for the sin in my life. I am sorry that my sin led You to the cross. Thank You for forgiving me and showing me that I need to forgive others. I pray that You help me to receive my husband's apologies, but also forgive him regardless of whether he is sorry or not. Holy Spirit, please continue to remove pride from my heart and anything else that would keep me from experiencing the power of forgiveness and reconciliation. Humble me, Lord, give me the courage to initiate reconciliation in my marriage.

In Jesus' name, AMEN!

Challenge:

Lean on God for the power to forgive others, trusting in Him to heal you. If you have any bitterness toward your husband go to him and reconcile.

Status Update:

"@unveiledwife Marriage is vulnerable because it is an intimate union between two sinners." #WifeAfterGod

Questions:

Why is it important to forgive others?

What things make it very difficult to forgive your husband?

Is there anything you should forgive your husband for currently?

FEAR NOT

ISAIAH 41:10, PSALM 56:3, MATTHEW 14:22-31,

DEUTERONOMY 5:29, JOSHUA 1:9, HEBREWS 11:1, 1 PETER 5:8

Fear is a distressing emotion caused by the presence or imminence of danger, whether that danger is actual or perceived. Synonyms of fear include afraid, anxiety, apprehension, dismay, doubt, dread, panic, scared, timidity, and worry. The world you live in is dark. The enemy prowls around looking for souls to snatch, families to disband, and marriages to destroy. Although there are many reasons your heart may fear, God commands in His Word not to fear, not to worry, not to be afraid. God does not want you to fear because it impairs your ability to live out extraordinary.

Matthew, one of the disciples, recalls a time when he was with a few other friends while the sea thrashed against their boat. They were terrified of the future, scared of what could happen to them. Through the raging storm, Jesus appeared to them walking on the water and their fears immediately got redirected as they thought they saw a ghost. Panic swirled around like a hurricane. Peter, realizing that the figure was Jesus, stepped out onto the sea; however, doubt caused him to fall beneath the current. Jesus was defying the laws of nature and changing history; Peter stood amidst a miracle and was scared right out of it! This interesting story reveals how fear can grip the heart, cloud the mind, and steal opportunities to experience audacious, awe-inspiring moments. But this story also reveals the faith required to get out of the boat in the first place. Don't let fear keep you from experiencing extraordinary. Instead, let faith and trust in God help you to get out of the boat and join God to do His will, regardless of the circumstances around you.

When you allow fear to control you, it can be debilitating as it exhausts you mentally, weakens you emotionally, and hinders you spiritually. Operating in fear spoils what God intends for you to encounter. For a wife, fear comes in many shapes and sizes. You may suffer the stress of fear when you doubt the love your husband has for you, leaving you feeling utterly insecure, or perhaps when you feel inclined to be transparent and honest, yet unknowing what will result of your vulnerability scares you from ever opening up.

The way in which fear is expressed can also affect your relationship with your husband, as evidence of it is woven through your words and how you say them. Fear, worry, and doubt intimidates you from the miracle of intimacy, while trying to convince you that God is not mighty enough to help, leading you to fall beneath the waves just as Peter did.

There is another aspect of fear that you must understand. Fear can also be defined as having reverence or awe. The only fear you should experience is through honoring God. Having high esteem for God is healthy fear. It requires humility, and it comes from your faith in Him. Faith is confidence in God. Faith will strengthen your soul, calm your mind, and renew your spirit. Faith screams, "God I trust you no matter what!" In faith you believe God's resources and power are unlimited. Faith gives you the courage to rely on God and to trust Him when He invites you to experience extraordinary. Operating in faith will fill your heart with God's peace and you will overflow with joy.

Faith will radically change the way you view your husband, too! Faith will lead you to communicate with your husband in amazing ways, intimate ways, where you won't be afraid of letting your husband know the real you. Faith will help you see your husband as God sees him, capable of transformation! As your confidence in God grows, what used to caution you as a risk becomes an incredible adventure. As you step out of the boat in faith, taking steps ever closer to God through His Son, Jesus Christ, even if you fall, He is there to help you! Do not fear and do not be dismayed, for God is with you!

Dear Lord,

I fear You! I honor You and I see You as mighty! Thank You for all of the ways you have made Yourself known to me, whether personally or through unbelievable stories shared throughout the Bible. I pray that I would not be afraid in this dark world. Please help me not to worry about finances, security, or any other circumstance that tempts me to doubt. I pray that my heart would only fear You! I pray that I would be completely confident in Your will for my life, that I would grow in faithfulness, and that I would trust in You more. I especially pray that fear would not seize my marriage. Please transform me so that I do not respond toward my husband in fear or worry. I desire to be a wife full of bravery and courage. I desire to be unveiled and transparent, making myself known to You and to my husband.

In Jesus' name, AMEN!

Challenge:

Don't let fear cripple your marriage. Find a special way to experience an adventure with your husband. This could be as simple as an intimate conversation! For creative date ideas visit: unveiledwife.com/date-ideas

Status Update:

"@unveiledwife My confidence is in God!" #WifeAfterGod

Questions:

In what instances has God invited you to do something, but you were too scared to follow through?

What things cause you to fear?

How does operating in fear affect your marriage?

A SUBMISSIVE HEART

MATTHEW 26:36-44, LUKE 22:44, GENESIS 2:21-23,

EPHESIANS 5:22-24, 1 PETER 3:1-2, 1 CORINTHIANS 11:3

Many women gasp when they hear the word submission. Body language speaks volumes when they cringe while making a face of disgust, almost as if even thinking of the word will provoke a fury of curses. The truth is that submission is a Biblical concept and without it there would be no salvation and no personal relationship with God.

You see, a very tender and beautiful act of submission occurred moments before Jesus was betrayed. He sat in the Garden of Gethsemane praying to His Father, His God, His everything. As blood dripped from His skin from the anguish of knowing what would be unleashed upon Him, Jesus fell face down on the ground and uttered these words, "My Father, if it be possible, let this cup pass from me; nevertheless, not as I will, but as you will." (Matthew 26:39, ESV)

Jesus knew what He was about to endure would be extremely difficult, so much that He asked God not to let it happen. However, Jesus prayed these same words to God three times, and three times He ended with "as you will." Despite everything He would go through, He trusted God and desired for God's will to be done. Jesus submitted to the will of His Father, His God, His everything. Through this powerful act of submission came salvation and reconciliation between God and mankind.

Submission is a posture of the heart, translated through behavior. It is a loving response to leadership and respecting the order which God has placed. God is a God of order and His Word defines His divine order. The head of Christ is God, the head of man is Christ, and the head of woman is man. Ephesians 5 sheds light specifically on the order in a marriage, explaining that a wife is to submit to her husband. This is God's order, that all wives submit to Him (God), first and foremost, and then to submit each to her own husband.

Order number one is that you submit to God's will above all.

Order number two is that you submit to your husband.
Submission does not suggest that a wife is a "doormat" as some tend to think. To be submissive does not mean that your opinions have no value or that you are less worthy of a person. Jesus was submissive to the Father

and yet He still voiced His thoughts through prayer. Likewise, as you live with a submissive heart, out of reverence for God and His Word, you remain worthy and remain with the freedom to share your heart with your husband, ultimately allowing your husband to lead you with the authority given to him through Christ.

Being a submissive wife is beautiful, as it reflects God's divine order. When a husband loves his wife like Christ loves and a wife submits to her husband, that reflection clearly represents God's grace-filled love story. The benefits in a marriage like this are extraordinary.

Having a submissive heart requires immense strength. Strength to be self-controlled, understanding, respectful, and loving. Strength to sacrifice things in this life that are meaningful, sometimes under circumstances that you will never be given an explanation for. Strength to trust God and to trust your husband.

A quote by Matthew Henry depicts the purpose of how God created woman, which states,

> *"Eve was not taken out of Adam's head to top him, neither out of his feet to be trampled on by him, but out of his side to be equal with him, under his arm to be protected by him, and near his heart to be loved by him."*

Woman was fashioned from the very side of man, designed with beauty and honor as man's beloved helper. God gave man the incredible gift of companionship through marriage, thus marking the beginning of an amazing love story. Although man and woman were both created in God's image, there is order, and God's ways are perfect.

Again, this does not imply that a wife is subject to subversive attacks by a controlling husband, nor does it mean that a wife is expected to compromise her faith in any way, for order number one always comes first, submission to God.

You have the extraordinary opportunity to fulfill God's order of submission through your relationship with Him, as well as through your relationship with your husband. Study the Word thoroughly and ask God to reveal to you what submission should look like in your relationship with Him and in your marriage. When a situation presents itself and you feel the conviction of the Holy Spirit guiding you to submit, remember that you do so out of reverence for Christ, motivated by a desire to fulfill God's will, not yours! If your husband does not submit to Christ, he obviously cannot lead you through love. Regardless, your part is to submit to your husband. Let faith be your motivator, faith that through your behavior you will win him over!

Submission is tender, graceful, and marvelous. May you be inspired to further explore what it means to have a submissive heart and the significance of why God established it in marriage.

As you act in obedience to God's order of submission, may your heart be filled with His peace and may your relationship with God and your husband experience extraordinary.

Dear Lord,

Thank You for sending Your Son, who endured so much anguish for the sake of Your will. Thank You, Jesus, for showing me how to submit to God, especially when it seems difficult. I pray that I would be able to submit to Your will like Jesus did. May Your Holy Spirit teach me what submission should look like in my marriage, and what my part is. Lord, give me a passionate desire to fulfill Your will. I pray for my husband, asking that he would always submit to You. I pray that he would lead me in love. Not my will, but Your's be done.

In Jesus' name, AMEN!

Challenge:
If there is a pending conflict or area in your marriage right now that requires you to be submissive, evaluate your heart and ask God what you should do. Go to your husband respectfully and explain to him your heart to be submissive.

Status Update:
"@unveiledwife I am able to submit to my husband out of reverence for Christ." #WifeAfterGod

Questions:
What do you think submission should look like in your marriage?

What hinders you from having a submissive heart?

How will your marriage change as you submit more to God?

WISDOM CALLS OUT

GENESIS 3:6, PROVERBS 9:10, PROVERBS 8,

1 CORINTHIANS 1:18-31, JAMES 1:5

Wisdom is a beautiful attribute of God. Wisdom witnessed the foundations of the Earth being formed, the seas filled, and the mountains placed. Wisdom is ancient, yet relevant. With truth on her lips, she calls out. Blessed are those who listen to her.

The beginning of wisdom is to fear God and hate evil. It is knowledge of what is right--not just knowing, but acting justly in that knowledge. Foolishness is knowing the truth, yet not acting on it. For example, Eve lived in a magnificent garden where she experienced an intimate relationship with God and her husband. God commanded Adam and Eve not to eat of a specific tree in the garden, a command of love and protection. Eve was deceived as she saw the fruit on that specific tree alluring, desiring to eat it so that she may gain wisdom. Eve's downfall was her pride, believing that she could find her own way to gain understanding and insight. She disregarded God's commandment by eating the fruit, while inviting her husband to sin along with her. It would have been better for Eve to ask God for wisdom, for true wisdom only comes from God. Although knowing the truth, she did not act on it. Foolishness filled her heart leading her to sin against her Creator, her God, her everything.

Have you ever thought you were being wise, confident that your way was the right way, yet you disregarded God's truth in order to do it? Eve may have been the first woman to have sinned, but she definitely wasn't the last. It is imperative to your relationship with God that you lean on Him to fill you with His wisdom so that you will know what is right and be able to stand strong, acting justly as God directs your paths. God's wisdom is precious. There is no earthly thing in this world you could desire that can compare to its value.

Soak up wisdom's call in Proverbs 8 and live a life dedicated to pursuing God's wisdom. Do not be deceived into thinking that your insights are great and mighty, because the truth has been made known through God's Word that God's wisdom lacks nothing and the wisdom of the world is merely foolishness. If you desire wisdom all you need to do is ask God and He will give it to you generously. Also, if you hunger for discernment and understanding, study the Gospel recorded by the disciples, because the power of God's wisdom was exemplified through the love story of Christ. As you strive to be more like Him, you will gain wisdom through the process of transformation.

Dear Lord,

I pray that You would give me Your wisdom. Anoint me with wisdom so that I may stand strong for what is right and that my actions reflect Your wisdom. I desire to operate in Your wisdom. Thank You Jesus, for being a great example of the power of wisdom! Transform me to be a woman and a wife who also exemplifies wisdom. Help me to see that wisdom is a treasure to be valued. Help me to see the positive effects it has on my marriage. I pray that I would listen intently as Your wisdom guides me.

In Jesus' name, AMEN!

Challenge:
Evaluate your marriage and write down any areas that you feel you need more wisdom. Pray over this list fervently and make notes when God gives you wisdom in those areas.

Status Update:
"@unveiledwife I am a wife striving to lean on God's wisdom and not my own." #WifeAfterGod

Questions:
In what instances have you acted on your own wisdom instead of God's wisdom?

What are some areas in your life that you desire to have more wisdom?

How will being a wife devoted to gaining God's wisdom impact your marriage?

DIAMOND IN THE ROUGH

EPHESIANS 4:14-16, 2 CORINTHIANS 4:6 -12

Diamonds have always been treasured as highly sought after gemstones throughout human history. Their uses range from pieces of fashion adornments to cutting blades. They are resilient, strong, and beautiful. Deep within the mantel of the Earth, diamonds are formed beneath the weight of the world. Through intense pressure in combination with extremely high temperatures, a diamond is produced. Hard-pressed and crushed on every side, rising to the surface through incidents such as volcanic eruptions, carried by scorching magma. Despite the harsh conditions required to form a diamond, its name is derived from an ancient Greek word meaning "unbreakable." This precious gem of utmost quality and concern is considered unbreakable.

You are like a diamond; however, your worth is far greater! As you journey through life you will endure harsh conditions. You may not literally know what it feels like to have the weight of the world pressing down on you, but there are times that you may feel as if it were. There are so many different pressures that you may face daily including some of the following:

- Society defines what is beautiful, demanding you to glamorize yourself to the world's standards before you are deemed attractive.

- Culture determines what weight or body shape is perfect, leaving not an inch of room for you to feel comfortable.

- Family members pull and tug for your time and attention, fighting for their rights to you on special occasions.

- Marital stressors become a source of unwanted conflict between you and your husband.

- Work zaps your energy no matter what it is, whether you have a boss or you are the boss.

- Church preaches principles of righteousness, yet provide no easy way of getting help with the hard stuff, the stuff others don't want to admit to because everyone else doesn't seem to struggle.

- You place unrealistic expectations on yourself, being your own worst critic and pressing thoughts of discouragement even further into your heart.

These are not truths, they are merely burdensome pressures found all around you at any given time.

Pressures to be better, to be a superwoman, a wife that manages perfectly or a mom who does it all. Ridicule, rules, standards, and unrealistic expectations: chains wrapped around your heart, pushing against your soul, forcing you to conform to the world. However, that is not the message found in the love story of Christ! Rather, His love says you are worth more and with Him you are unbreakable!

Despite how you may feel at the end of the day, as you cling to hope in God, you know it will all be okay. Society, family, and others may be cunning as they try to compress you to their wills, their ideals, their desires or their expectations, which may lead to conflict, but remember you are a diamond being processed through transformation. Hard pressed on every side, perplexed, persecuted and struck down, but never destroyed! Persevere, my friend!

Persevering in your relationship with God will help you to withstand the weight of the world. Persevering in your relationship with your husband will help you to withstand the extreme heat of the flaming arrows of the enemy. Like a diamond endures through time resulting in an exquisite sought after gem, you can endure every season and circumstance allowing each one to refine you, resulting in an exquisite God-fearing woman who is worthy, far more than diamonds, you are worthy! You are resilient, you are strong, you are beautiful!

Dear Lord,

There are so many pressures in my life. I feel heavy burdens at times and I also feel insecure that I don't always measure up to people's standards. I pray that You remind me daily to find hope in You, to rely on You and to trust what You say about me. Your opinion is truly the only one that matters! Thank You for being my source of strength to persevere, my everything. May You continue to transform me into the woman You created me to be. Help me to see myself as beautiful. May Your Holy Spirit guide me through every season, every circumstance, every pressure and every moment of intensity. I pray that I can be a wife who endures for the sake of her marriage. Please bless my husband and release him of the burdens of this world.

In Jesus' name, AMEN!

Challenge:
Write down a list of the biggest pressures you feel on a daily basis and how they affect you. Next to each one listed, write about the pressure in a positive light, as if it were an encouragement from God.

For example:
Pressure - I feel like I will never be as beautiful as any celebrity. I have too many freckles and blemishes.
Truth - God thinks I am beautiful. He created me and accepts every freckle and every part of me that the world says is a flaw.

Status Update:
"@unveiledwife The pressures of this world cannot destroy me if I place my hope in God." #WifeAfterGod

Questions:
What pressures do women face currently?

What types of pressures make it difficult for you to have joy in your marriage?

Why is it easier to believe what the world says about you, than it is to believe what God says about you?

WHO YOU ARE CALLED TO BE

1 CORINTHIANS 6:12-20, MATTHEW 22:37-40,

1 PETER 1:15-16 , PHILIPPIANS 1:6

With the inevitable pressures in this world capable of bearing down on you to the point of exhaustion, it is crucial that you know who you are called to be according to your Maker, your God, your incredible source of hope and strength. He reveals who you are called to be throughout His Word. He guides you to be a virtuous woman who upholds Biblical standards of truth! Before you allow society or even marriage to define you as a woman, you need to have confidence in the truth of what God calls you to be. Love God's Word, meditate on it, memorize it, saturate your soul with it, and relish in the beauty of His call.

There is not a master list highlighting who you are called to be, rather there are callings found woven throughout the Bible. For example, in 1 Corinthians God calls you to honor Him with your body. Your body is a temple for the Holy Spirit! God desires for you to honor Him with your body, reflecting His love story through your actions. Instead of worrying about what size jeans you fit into, God wants you to be aware of the condition of your heart. Instead of concerning yourself with stretch marks, wrinkles, or scars, God wants you to repent from sin. Honor God with your body by being healthy, not obsessed, confident, not insecure, accepting, not dissatisfied. Honor God with your body by using it as a vessel to do your part according to His will!

Another example of who you are called to be is found in 1 Peter, which states that you should be Holy as God is Holy. This means that you are set apart from the world, despite being submerged in it. Your light will shine bright like an illuminated lamp. As you strive to be more like Jesus, the Holy Spirit sanctifies you. Instead of indulging in sin to self-satisfy, you will become a new creation in Christ--you will become refined, Holy.

You are also called to be loving. There is no doubt that God has called you to be loving. In fact, Matthew recorded Jesus explaining that the two greatest commandments are to love God and love others. Instead of focusing on yourself, be love-focused toward others. Find joy in understanding the depths of God's love, and then take the initiative to express that love to others. Obedience to these two commandments will lead you to experience extraordinary!

Honor God with your body, be holy, and love extravagantly. These are just three of the many examples mentioned in God's Word of who you are called to be. Each calling serves as a guide to help you define who God created you to be. Understanding who God calls you to be and striving to fulfill each call, will grow you closer to God, especially as you search His Word and meditate on it. Your relationship with your husband will also deepen and strengthen as you are transformed in Christ. Your husband will be blessed through the positive changes occurring in your actions, attitudes, and words. Don't hesitate to explore who God calls you to be, and don't hesitate to answer the call by accepting His truth and acting in wisdom to live out each one!

Dear Lord,

Thank You for taking the time to show me who You call me to be. Thank You for Your Holy Word which directs my steps. I pray that I would passionately explore all the different calls You share in Your Word and commit to living them out. I understand that by being faithful in this way You will transform my character to reflect yours. I pray that my relationship with You and my marriage to my husband will continue to grow and be blessed. I pray over my husband right now. I pray he begins to discern who You have called him to be. Give him curiosity to learn like I am. Holy Spirit please fill his heart with your goodness and power, direct his steps, and transform his heart.

In Jesus' name, AMEN!

Challenge:

Spend time searching the Bible for scriptures to support who you are called to be in Christ. For a list of scripture references visit: unveiledwife.com/gods-call

Status Update:

"@unveiledwife I am a wife called to be a virtuous woman who upholds Biblical standards of truth."
#WifeAfterGod

Questions:

Who does God call you to be?

How will your marriage be impacted as you live out these calls?

What is one call that you need to spend more time working on?

PRAYER FOR YOU

COLOSSIANS 4:2, HEBREWS 5:7, MATTHEW 6:9-13

Prayer is an intimate way of communicating with your God. Through prayer you can thank Him, ask of Him, and share with Him all of the details of your life. There is nothing that is too big that would be impossible for Him to handle and nothing that is too small that He would want you to leave out. He yearns to hear from you, just like a loving father would bend down to listen to his child. You are a child of God and He will listen to you.

Prayer will draw you close to God as you converse with Him throughout the day. There are no special words or specific order to which you need to pray, although Jesus does provide a model to teach you how to pray with the example in Matthew 6. In addition, as you have journeyed through this devotional, you have had the opportunity to participate in prayer through the ones provided at the end of each chapter. Each prayer serves to encourage you and guide you in how to pray for yourself, as well as for your husband!

It is extremely important that you devote yourself to prayer daily. Establishing fervor for daily prayer is part of God's will for you, and by doing so you are submitting to Him. Praying for yourself is significant because it humbles you as thankfulness and appreciation flow from your heart. As you pray for transformation of your character, you will begin to see change, and when you inquire for understanding you will gain wisdom. It is good for you to pray for yourself, that you may align your heart with God's, and for protection from the enemy. Revealing your heart to God through prayer is the most essential way to experience extraordinary intimacy with God. Nurturing great communication is vital for any thriving relationship.

Be intentional about pursing time every day to pray for yourself. Share with your God, your everything, about your life, about your emotions, about the condition of your heart, about needs that you have, about your appreciation, about answered prayers, about change you are experiencing, about change you desire to experience, and about His will. You can pray out loud or you can pray in your heart, God hears both! Also, be intentional about listening to God. He will respond to you, perhaps in different and unique ways, but He will respond. You are His beloved daughter and He wants to hear from you!

Dear Lord,

Thank You for the gift of prayer. I value being able to come and share my heart with You. I am also blessed to be able to lift my request to You! Prayer builds my faith in You, it draws me close to You, and it reminds me to seek after You daily. Please put passion in my heart to pray every day. Holy Spirit please help me to understand prayer better, and give me the discipline to spend quality time talking to You. I pray that You continue to transform my character. May You mold me into the woman and the wife You created me to be. Fill me with Your wisdom, Your patience, Your kindness, and Your great love. I pray that I would mirror Your image and that others would ask me why I have joy. I pray that in that moment You would give me the courage and the words to share Your incredible love story, Your Gospel! Give me ears to hear You! I pray protection over me from the enemy. Guard my mind from temptation, help me to stand firm in faith, and defend me against this dark world. Thank You for giving me so much! All I need is You! Lord, may Your will be done in me and through me.

In Jesus' name, AMEN!

Challenge:
Take time throughout the day to pray for yourself.

Status Update:
"@unveiledwife Prayer is the most essential way to cultivate intimacy with God." #WifeAfterGod

Questions:
Why is it important for you to pray every day?

How has the guided prayers in this devotional impacted you?

In what ways can you increase quality prayer time with God?

PRAYER FOR YOUR HUSBAND

1 THESSALONIANS 5:16-18, JAMES 5:13-16,

EPHESIANS 6:12

Praying for your husband is necessary for a God-centered marriage. As you focus on praying for your husband, God will move in powerful ways. Submitting to God through prayer aligns your heart, your desires, and your will to the heart of your Almighty God. When you pray specifically for your husband, you are inviting God to enact His precious will in your marriage.

If you are praying to see change in your husband, be sure that your motives are not selfish, and that the change you desire to see is so that your husband will draw closer to God. Be intentional about praying for your husband to experience extraordinary intimacy with God, for him to learn more about God's ways, and for him to lead like Jesus. May your intentions be based on faith that your husband will mature into the man and husband God created him to be.

Praying for your husband daily is of utmost importance. Prayer requires a heart of humility, so by devoting yourself to daily praying for your husband, you are keeping your heart softened toward him and remaining mindful of his needs. Thus, cultivating an atmosphere of intimacy, where selfishness and pride cannot tear down your marriage.

When you pray for your husband, thank God for him, lift up any needs he may have, and always implore God's protection over him. This world is full of evil, especially in the many ways media exploits love and sex. Ask God to cover your husband so that he would not be exposed to the perverse things in this world, including the temptations which lurk. May you always remember that there is a battle going on, it is not against flesh and blood, but against the forces of the enemy. Prayer is your weapon to defend the cause of Christ, His love story, and your love story. This battle is constantly tugging at your husband, trying to weaken him and ruin your relationship with him. Stand in God's strength, fight for your husband, and use your weapon of prayer diligently. Pray for your husband's soul, insist that God blesses him, sends him encouragements, and fills his heart with joy. Take advantage of the opportunity you have to beseech your King and Commander for the very life of your beloved husband.

Dear Lord,

Thank You for my husband. Thank You for his heart, his health, and his love for me. I lift him up to You and ask that You would bless him. Use people around him, including me to affirm him. I pray that he would be encouraged to seek after You and lead like Jesus. May Your Holy Spirit transform his character so that he reflects You, Lord. Help him improve in the areas he is weak, and continue to strengthen him each day. May he draw close to You Lord, and may Your will be evident in his life. I pray against the powers of this dark world, I pray against temptations, I pray against the schemes of the enemy that try to attack my husband. I pray for protection in Jesus' name! Reveal to him Your wisdom and Your truths. May his soul know You well. I pray that I can help him and inspire him everyday.

In Jesus' name, AMEN!

Challenge:
Spend time praying for your husband. Share with God why you are thankful for him, lift up any needs he may have, pray for his character to reflect Christ, and petition God to protect him.

Status Update:
"@unveiledwife I am devoted to praying for my husband." #WifeAfterGod

Questions:
How will praying for your husband positively impact your marriage?

What are some specific things you know your husband needs prayer for?

How will praying for your husband draw you closer to him and to God?

PRAYER FOR YOUR MARRIAGE

ECCLESIASTES 4:12, MATTHEW 18:20, MARK 10:16,

ROMANS 12:10-13

The relationship between a husband and wife is
founded on incredible love. However, the marriage
relationship is not impenetrable, bulletproof, nor is it
immune to the influence of this world. Although the
love between a husband and wife is powerful, marriage
will always be vulnerable and fragile. You must take
action to protect your marriage and build it up strong,
centered on God. You can do this through prayer.
Praying for your marriage every day will encourage
your faithfulness, bring peace to your home, and it will
give God the opportunity to fulfill His will. As you and
your husband submit to God through prayer, He will
lead you, He will direct your steps, and He will have the
joy of experiencing life with you.

Praying with your husband is one of the most intimate

experiences you will ever encounter, because the two of you are going before God together. Jesus says that when two or more are gathered in His name He is present. Therefore, when you and your husband come together in His name to pray, He is there! Building a solid foundation of prayer in your marriage should be a priority, as this is what centers your marriage on God.

If your husband refuses to pray with you, be still and trust God. Pray on your own that your husband's heart will be passionate about prayer, having faith that you will one day be able to experience prayer with him. Sometimes praying out loud with another person can be difficult. Remember that prayer requires humility and that as you practice praying with your husband it will become more comfortable.

There will never be a lack of things to pray for with your husband. Designate time every day to thank God and to lift your requests up to Him. Pray for the day and the plans you two have made, pray that your hearts are sensitive toward God and toward each other, pray over struggles that tempt you, pray protection over your relationship, and always pray that God would teach you how to love better. Invite God to be a part of your lives, to walk alongside you, and on difficult days ask Him to carry you. Prayer is phenomenally effective. When you and your husband are having a hard day, stop everything and go to God together in prayer! Devote yourselves to prayer for your marriage and experience transformation together!

Dear Lord,

Thank You for the gift of marriage. It is such a blessing to have the opportunity to experience intimacy through prayer with my husband. I pray that my husband would have passion to pray with me and that we would devote ourselves to it daily. Help us to center our marriage on You, Lord. Please give us the words to say when we pray and reveal to us what things need prayer. I pray that our marriage would mature as you transform our hearts. Increase our intimacy, help us manage our finances, may You free us from sin that entangles us, and may your will be done through us. May we experience extraordinary in our marriage.

In Jesus' name, AMEN!

Challenge:
Ask your husband to pray with you over your marriage. Here are some areas of marriage that you can pray over:

- Intimacy
- Restoration
- Trust
- Forgiveness
- Children
- Finances
- Tithe

- Health
- Family
- In-Laws
- Job
- Housing
- Hobbies

If your husband refuses your invitation to pray together, find a quiet place and pray by yourself. Pray for your marriage and for your husband.

Status Update:
"@unveiledwife I am devoted to praying for my marriage." #WifeAfterGod

Questions:
How does praying with your husband build a God-centered marriage?

What keeps you from asking your husband to pray with you?

What changes need to be made so that you can pray with your husband for your marriage on a daily basis?

GIFTS OF THE SPIRIT

JOHN 14:25-27, ROMANS 12:3-8,

1 CORINTHIANS 12:1-11, 1 CORINTHIANS 12:27,

1 CORINTHIANS 13:8

The Holy Spirit is God's Spirit. When Jesus ascended into heaven, God sent the Holy Spirit to dwell within faithful believers, to teach and to remind them of all that Jesus said. The Holy Spirit is an advocate for you, to teach you the wisdom of God, to comfort you in times of need, and to convict you when you need reproof. The Holy Spirit also comes bearing gifts, evidences of the power of God. Paul mentions the gifts of the Spirit in Corinthians and again in Romans.

It is important for you to know about the gifts of the Spirit so that you may have confidence when God invites you to join Him to participate in His work. You see, it is not by your own strength that you operate to fulfill God's will, it is the very power of God that enables you!

Awesomely, the Holy Spirit is interconnected through believers, a common thread that unifies the family of God as one body. And although there may be different projects or different types of work going on in the lives of believers, take heart knowing that it is the same God who is at work. The Holy Spirit distributes gifts to glorify God as others are blessed through His work in you. The ultimate goal and miracle of His work is that nonbelievers would come to know Him, so it is crucial that you do not become conceited in the gifts you are given, rather give God all the glory for what is done. Remember all gifts are empowered by the Holy Spirit to do God's work!

At the end of 1 Corinthians 12 Paul challenges believers to desire the greater gifts, then leads into the chapter on true love. Love is the greatest gift ever given and ever received. Love is God's motivation and reason for working in the first place. Love is the greatest gift of all. With the power and the gifts of the Holy Spirit your confidence in God's ability to use you should increase dramatically.

One of the most influential ways God will invite you to join in His work will be in your marriage. You and your husband have a unique opportunity to help each other mature in your walks with God and to work alongside each other in God's will. For instance, the gifts of the Holy Spirit mentioned in Romans can be shared in your marriage through examples of serving one another, encouraging one another, and showing one another mercy, all which are motivated by the greatest gift of all: love. By allowing the Holy Spirit to lead you in this way, your relationship with God will grow closer as you lean on Him for the strength to do any one of those things, and through your actions you will grow closer to your husband!

The Holy Spirit is a gift, an advocate to help you navigate through your marriage, through other relationships, and empowers you to join God in His work. Appreciate the value in such an incredible gift and thank God for not having to endure this life alone.

Dear Lord,

Thank You for the gift of Your Holy Spirit who is my advocate. Thank You for sending me Your Holy Spirit and for the good gifts You give. I pray for the wisdom to understand each of these gifts and to discern which ones You have distributed to me to do Your work. Thank You especially for the gift of love. Help me to fully comprehend the impact of love, sincere, genuine love. The kind of love that You define in Your Word! I give You all the glory Lord, for the work in my life! I know it is You who empowers me, it is You who teaches me, it is You who comforts me and reproves me. Thank You for transforming me into the woman You created me to be. I pray that my heart is open and that I recognize the work You are doing in and through my marriage. When You invite me to bless my husband by serving him or encouraging him, please show me how, humble me, and give me the courage to follow through. I also pray that my husband grows confidently in You. Use me Lord, to help him and to draw him close to You. I pray that I would share Your gift of great love with my husband and with others.

In Jesus' name, AMEN!

Challenge:

Read 1 Corinthians 13:4-8 about the definition of love. If there is an area you tend to struggle with toward your husband such as patience or trust be intentional about letting God help you be better. Visit unveiledwife. com/what-is-love-series and find the article that talks about that which you struggle with and complete the challenge found in the article.

Status Update:

"@unveiledwife It is not by my strength that I operate to do God's will, It is the very power of God that enables me." #WifeAfterGod

Questions:

Why did God send His Holy Spirit?

Why is love the greatest gift?

How can the gifts of the Holy Spirit positively affect your marriage?

THE PARTS OF MARRIAGE

GENESIS 2:24, 1 CORINTHIANS 12:12-27,

EPHESIANS 5:28-33

There is a profound mystery wrapped up in the relationship between Christ and the Church when compared to the relationship between a husband and wife. The two love stories have a phenomenal ability to mirror each other. So when Biblical concepts are illustrated creatively throughout God's Word to expound understanding and draw one closer to God, sometimes that same illustration can be viewed in light of marriage to help a husband or wife understand God's design of their relationship. This truth is what spurred the development of this devotional!

One of those illustrations, mentioned in the New Testament, uses the intricately contrived human body. The example Paul chose simply explains how parts make up a whole. A foot, an ear, an eye, they are all individual parts, working alongside other parts to fulfill their function and to make up the whole human body. Likewise, as a Christian you become a member of Christ's body, working alongside other believers to fulfill God's will. Although everyone is given a different distribution of gifts by the Holy Spirit, they work in unity and in obedience to God. As a Christian, God has called you to love and respect the body of Christ; treating one another with respect, encouraging one another with affirmation, and caring for one another with the knowledge that each part is valuable, each part is worthy.

All the more, when a husband and wife enter into a covenantal relationship they become one flesh. Just as a body takes care of its parts, and Jesus takes care of His body, so a husband and wife are responsible to take care of each other as they now represent one flesh, one body, one marriage.

You and your husband have been joined together in Holy matrimony. One flesh. You are accountable for your part and your husband is accountable for his. Although you are individual beings decorated with colorful preferences, traits, opinions, and characteristics, God designed you to be able to work together in unity. However, a thriving marriage built in unity requires humbleness, selflessness, and unconditional love. With these three tender attributes fueling your heart, you will never grow weary of trying--trying to work as one with your husband, trying to do good to him all the days of his life, trying to honor God by respecting your husband, and trying to pray for your husband in faith that God will captivate his heart.

In 1 Corinthians 12:26 it encourages you to be aware of how the body as a whole is doing; if one part suffers, every part suffers with it, or if one part is honored the body rejoices. If your husband is suffering, stand beside him, help carry him along with compassion in your heart. If your husband is honored, receives acclaim, or perhaps a promotion, celebrate with him and be his cheerleader. Be a wife eager to fulfill your husband's needs, knowing that the result will benefit your marriage as a whole. Never stop trying, never stop loving, never give up.

Dear Lord,

Your Holy Word is inspiring. Thank You for the illustrations You present to help me in understanding Your ways and Your design. You created me and You created marriage. I need to trust You more and trust how Your Word guides me in my role as a Christian wife. I pray that as a member of the body of Christ I am diligent in fulfilling Your will. You have purposed me with gifts to further Your great Kingdom, to spread Your incredible love. Please help me to see the whole body of Christ and honor each part, every person. I also pray that my husband and I learn to operate as one flesh. Give me eyes to see when my husband is hurting or when he needs affirmation or when he just needs rejoicing. I desire a thriving marriage, a God-centered marriage, a marriage built with unity. May You bless my husband in great ways, use me to fulfill his needs, and draw us close as husband and wife. I pray that we would experience the joining of one flesh through intimacy.

In Jesus' name, AMEN!

Challenge:

Find one way to bless the body of Christ, whether it is encouraging someone or fulfilling a need. Also, do one thing to bless your body, your marriage.

Status Update:

"@unveiledwife My husband and I are one flesh, one body, one marriage." #WifeAfterGod

Questions:

How does 1 Corinthians 12:26 play out in your marriage? Describe examples.

What things hinder you from comforting your husband when he needs it or celebrating with him when something good happens?

Just like you take care of your body daily, what are some things you can do to take care of your marriage daily to maintain it and keep it healthy?

FRUITFULNESS

GALATIANS 5:22-26, JOHN 15:1-11

A lively breeze whipped through the windows of the family minivan. A young girl's hair twirled through the air as her mom drove away from the sunset. It was the girl's favorite time of day as she imagined God painting the sky in vibrant bursts of color and everything around her seemed to glow. The yellow hue of the sun was striking, as if her world had been dipped in gold. All of a sudden her hair fell against her shoulders, her mom had stopped the van, got out, and headed toward a wooden fence. Hanging over the fence was a lush green tree with random spots of red scattered about its leaves. Within seconds her mom was back in the van, starting up the engine, but she wasn't empty handed. Her mom held up a round piece of fruit that was a beautiful rich, dark red. Holding it up with pride her mother said with enthusiasm as if she discovered treasure, "This is a pomegranate!" The young girl had never seen a pomegranate before, all she could imagine was how it looked inside and how it tasted.

When they arrived home, the young girl, eager to explore more about this fruit, followed her mom into the kitchen. Her mom grabbed a knife and split the fruit down the middle. The girl did not expect to see small round balls stuffed full inside. Taking a few pieces between her tiny fingers she popped the balls into her mouth, flavor exploded.

It was adventures such as this that survived as memories for the little girl. Something as sweet as fruit made a huge impact in her life, stirring her curiosity and satisfying her hunger. She tasted goodness and it left a lasting impression on her heart.

You can also have an incredible, lasting impression on the lives of those around you. Your fruitfulness can draw others in and leave them feeling satisfied and refreshed. Fruitfulness in your life is produced when you abide in Christ. To abide means you submit to Him in reverence, you accept His truth, and you remain steadfast. As you abide in Christ, you are transformed by God's power, therefore able to bear the fruit of the Holy Spirit. This kind of fruit is created in your heart when you chose to live according to God's ways. Joy, peace, patience, kindness, goodness, faithfulness, gentleness and self-control--a beautiful combination of complementing fruit, evidence of a righteous character.

You will be recognizable by this fruit as they are expressed through your actions. With it comes impact, especially in your marriage. As you do your part and abide in Christ, your husband receives the benefit of tasting the goodness of God. This kind of fruitfulness creates an atmosphere of thick love, a place where intimacy thrives. You have impact, you have impression, you...despite your sins, your faults, and your failures. Abide in Christ and you will experience extraordinary!

Dear Lord,

I pray that You would help me to abide in Christ, to relish in my relationship with You, to submit to You, to accept Your truth and to remain in You always. I pray that my character is transformed to reflect Yours. May joy, peace, patience, kindness, goodness, faithfulness, gentleness, and self-control be evident in my life. May they be abundant in my life. I hope that others around me would feel refreshed because of the fruit I produce. I pray that my husband would be blessed as I respond to him with a heart full of these fruits. If there is a specific fruit that I need more of, please reveal it to me and then show me how I can produce an increase.

In Jesus' name, AMEN!

Challenge:
Spend time relishing in your relationship with Christ. Get your favorite piece of fruit and pair it with a fruit of the Holy Spirit that you need more of, especially toward your husband, and as you eat it let it serve as a symbol of your commitment to pray for that fruit to increase in your heart.

Status Update:
"@unveiledwife Fruitfulness of character is produced when I abide in Christ." #WifeAfterGod

Questions:
What fruit of the Spirit do you feel you are lacking?

How will an intentional increase in fruit production positively affect your relationship with God and your husband?

DAY 26

HIDING FROM GOD

GENESIS 3:8-13, ROMANS 3:23, JAMES 4:17, 1 JOHN 1:8-10

Sin is an offense, a violation of disobedience against
God. The first story of God's relationship with man
reveals the ugliness of sin and its detriment. Adam
and Eve ate from the only tree in the Garden of Eden
that God commanded them to stay away from. God's
intentions of such a command was to protect Adam
and Eve's relationship with Him. However, they gave
into the temptation of sin, transgressing against their
Maker, their friend, their God. The intimate union
between them and God was severed. They felt the
weight of shame knowing that they had wronged God,
leading them to hide from His presence.

Have you ever felt the weight of shame? Has your
sin ever led you to hide from God or hide from your
spouse? Retreating to find a hiding spot further injures
the wound of being severed intimately. Perhaps you
don't actually hide as Adam and Eve did in the garden,
but do you hide sin in your heart? Do you keep your sin

hidden from those that you love? Fear is the motivation for hiding. Fear of the repercussions, fear of opinions cast about you, fear about losing love or intimacy, fear of being completely known, fear of feeling weak, fear of feeling hurt or pain, fear of having to repent, and the list of fears could continue.

Aside from hiding, do you justify your behavior? Do you place the blame on others? When Adam was asked why he sinned, he blamed his wife, then Eve turned around and blamed the serpent. Justifying your behavior or blaming others as the fault is an illusion you convince yourself to believe, manifested to protect yourself from being wrong, from experiencing consequence, and from acknowledging your imperfection. The motivator is pride. The combination of sin, fear, and pride is a deadly force that will keep the wounds of severed intimacy raw and infected, resistant against healing and restoration.

God never stopped loving Adam and Eve despite their sin, yet there were consequences because of their behavior. When you sin there will be consequences, but there is also opportunity to heal through repentance and forgiveness. Remember God has given you the ministry of reconciliation through Christ's sacrifice! Sin may sever your intimacy with God or with your husband, but if you are humble, courageous, and you sincerely repent, meaning you regret sinning and commit to not doing those sins again, you can achieve the rebuilding of intimacy. You must come out of hiding, realize you are accountable for your actions, and you must be willing to initiate the process of reconciliation. This is your part in the story.

Dear Lord,

I do not want to hide from Your presence. I do not want sin, fear, or pride to destroy my relationship with You or my marriage. Please heal me and free me from the bondage of sin. If there is anything that I am hiding from You please help me to bring it to the surface of my heart. May Your light illuminate in me, pushing out any darkness. I pray against shame, I pray against guilt, and I pray against the past that looms over my heart ready to remind me that I am not good enough. I pray that I am a woman and a wife courageous enough to rebuild intimacy and initiate reconciliation. Holy Spirit aid me and equip me to fulfill my part of the story.

In Jesus' name, AMEN!

Challenge:

If you are struggling with sin, take responsibility, go to God first and seek reconciliation. Then go to your husband, also pursue reconciliation and then invite him to help keep you accountable to righteousness.

Status Update:

"@unveiledwife Sin, fear and pride will keep the wounds of severed intimacy resistant to healing." #WifeAfterGod

Questions:

Have you and your husband ever been afraid of God or hid from Him because of sin?

How has sin affected your intimacy with God or intimacy with your husband?

Is there anything in your life right now that you are hiding from God or from your husband because of shame, fear, or pride?

INTIMACY WITH GOD

GENESIS 3:8-9, MATTHEW 26:20-30,

ROMANS 8:37-39, PSALMS 63:1-8, 1 PETER 4:8,

JOHN 17:22-23

Intimacy is the affection and love shared within a personal relationship with another. It is the pursuit of knowing the deepest part of someone, while revealing the deepest part of you; an interchange which fosters connection and acceptance. True intimacy requires vulnerability as those involved make themselves known through revealing very personal things encompassing the whole self: physically, spiritually, emotionally, and mentally. Intimacy is the process of drawing closer to another. Intimacy is making yourself known to another.

God has designed you in His image with the capacity for intimacy. Why? Because God desires an intimate relationship with His creation. Genesis 3 acknowledges that God was walking in the garden, seeking man and his wife. God was pursuing an intimate, love relationship with them. In the cool of the day, as if wooing them with His affections, God appeared in the garden desiring to walk side-by-side Adam and Eve. He called out to them, yet they were afraid and hid because they had sinned. Sin breaks fellowship with God and hinders intimacy.

Just as God pursued Adam and Eve, He pursues you. God loves you more than you will ever comprehend. His love motivates His pursuit. He will use everything around you to point your heart to His. He will woo you with His affection and He desires to walk by your side. No matter how old you are, no matter what you have done in your past, no matter what sin you have committed, God loves you, and His love is persistently pursuing an intimate relationship with you.

Unfortunately, sin has crept into the hearts of God's creation, making it impossible to be intimate with God. However, God sent His Son, Jesus Christ, to be the atoning sacrifice so that His creation may be reconciled to Himself. Even after His creation sinned against Him, God still pursued an intimate love relationship with His people. His pursuit continued even after Christ's resurrection when He sent the Holy Spirit as a comforter, to dwell inside believers. Sin hinders intimacy, but forgiveness restores it. Sin hinders intimacy, but love redeems it.

When there is sin in your life it breaks fellowship and intimacy with God. You need to make sure that you confess and repent of your sin so that you may continue in an intimate relationship with God. A personal relationship with God begins with prayer and communicating to Him your heart, all of your heart. Do not let the past or the possibility of future sins keep you from experiencing amazing intimacy with your Creator. He believes you are worthy--you always have been, and you always will be. God undoubtedly and audaciously loves you, and He desires to get to know you all the more through sharing intimate moments with Him!

Just before Jesus' final day as a man on Earth, He had a very intimate moment with His disciples. Sitting among the handful of men who courageously followed Him, He illustrated to them what He was about to endure. Although the men did not understand at the time, Jesus did not hesitate to share. Picking up a piece of bread and a cup of wine He explained how the two represent His body and His blood, which were going to be broken and poured out for the forgiveness of sins. Today, God still uses that one act of intimacy to experience closeness with His creation. Through communion, believers eat a piece of bread and drink either juice or wine to remember what Christ endured for the purpose of reconciliation and the restoration of intimacy. Partaking in communion is one way that you can experience intimacy with God.

There are many ways to cultivate intimacy with God. He has already been pursuing you...just respond. Compliment His extravagant gestures and tell Him how they make you feel. Walk among gardens and appreciate all that He has created for your enjoyment. Share with Him why life is overwhelming at times, cry out to Him, let Him know if you are tired or angry. Confess sins that entangle you, petition for freedom and healing. Talk to your God and listen to your God. Sometimes just be still. The more often you lean on Him, rely on Him, and trust in Him, you will become familiar with Him and you will know Him, without a doubt you will know Him.

Dear Lord,

Thank You for passionately pursuing me. Your creative ways of showing me Your love are insanely beautiful. Please open the eyes of my heart so I will never miss any of Your kind affections. Thank You for wanting to get to know me more. I pray that I would have the courage to unveil myself before You. Meet with me daily, speak to me, and open my ears so that I may hear. Help me to be grateful for all the ways You woo me. I pray that our relationship grows. I desire to have an intimate relationship with You, God, and I desire to know You more. As the world keeps spinning, I pray that I intentionally make time to be still and meditate on your precious Word and communicate to You through fervent prayer. If there is sin in my life, please reveal it to me so that I may repent. I do not want anything to break my fellowship with You. Thank You, God, for loving me. I love you.

In Jesus' name, Amen!

Challenge:
Talk to God about all the wonderful ways He is pursuing you and thank Him for each one! Also, grab a piece of bread and a cup of wine or juice and experience communion with God. Thank Him for sending His only Son and thank Jesus for all that He endured for you.

Status Update:
"@unveiledwife I am on a journey to make myself known to God and to know Him better!" #WifeAfterGod

Questions:
In what ways do feel God might be pursuing an intimate relationship with you?

What areas of your heart have you kept from God?

How will an intimate relationship with God affect your marriage?

What is one way you can pursue God right now?

INTIMACY IN MARRIAGE

GENESIS 2:24, 1 CORINTHIANS 7:1-5,

1 JOHN 4:7-8

God created you in His image, an intimate being fashioned for relationship. He passionately pursues you with an invitation to join Him in a love relationship and He desires that you get to experience the richness of intimacy with others, specifically your husband. Your marriage represents the intimate relationship of Jesus and His Bride, the Church. The two love stories mirror each other in a mysterious, yet profound way. Although maintaining personal relationships can face challenges at times, you were made for it, designed with a need for it!

There is a connotation floating around in society that defines intimacy solely as sex. Although sex is an intimate experience that a husband and wife share together, true intimacy is more than just sex. Many people misinterpret the word intimacy, therefore missing out on the extraordinary power of it. Intimacy is making yourself known. God's purpose for marriage is for a husband and wife to experience a love relationship, where they passionately pursue each other daily, where the ups and downs draw them closer together, a place where true intimacy thrives.

Similar to your relationship with God, cultivating intimacy in marriage requires vulnerability. The more effort you and your husband expend to reveal yourselves deeply to each other, the more familiar you two will become. In so doing, your marriage will be blessed as your marital foundation is fortified.

Intimacy in marriage is part of God's great design. Genesis 2 recognizes that a husband and wife become one flesh. This concept of oneness was deliberate and significant; a husband and wife are to humble themselves for the sake of the other and to seek the benefit of the whole of them. As you and your husband live as one flesh, intimacy is experienced and love is lived out.

There are many ways to increase intimacy in marriage and nurture oneness, including some of the following:

- Communicating through honest conversations
- Initiate sexual intimacy
- Confess sins
- Pray together
- Go on date nights

- Pursue each other passionately
- Talk about goals and dreams
- Serve each other
- Bless each other

Building a healthy, joyful, God-centered marriage where intimacy thrives is attainable, but it takes time and energy. It builds up over time as trust, confidence and faithfulness are produced. You are responsible to fulfill your part and your husband is responsible for his. Your marriage will reach this fulfillment when both of you are working together toward oneness. However, God calls you to remain steadfast in doing your part. Do it regardless of whether your husband is doing his. Let love motivate you and fuel your heart to persevere. Your marriage is worth it, it will always be worth it.

Dear Lord,

I lift up my marriage to You in thankfulness. You know every detail of my marriage, what my husband and I have been through, and where we are currently. May You help us to increase our intimacy. I desire to know my husband deeply, but I also know that requires that I am vulnerable and honest with him. Please give me the courage to open up to my husband, to talk about important matters of the heart, to share each other's goals, and to encourage each other in great ways. I pray that I can be a wife willing to initiate sexually, willing to serve joyfully, and willing to love extravagantly. May Your Holy Spirit ignite a fire in our marriage, a desire to draw close to one another and to become familiar with each other. I pray that You would soften my husband's heart toward me. Bless him with a desire to get to know me more. I pray against the enemy from stealing moments of intimacy, distracting us with selfish desires and tempting us away from experiencing true intimacy. May our love story and our intimacy reveal Your power so that others may be encouraged.

In Jesus' name, AMEN!

Challenge:

From the list mentioned in this chapter, choose one way to initiate intimacy in your marriage today. For more ways to initiate intimacy in marriage please visit: unveiledwife.com/intimacy

Status Update:

"@unveiledwife I commit to initiating true intimacy with my husband." #WifeAfterGod

Questions:

How does intimacy in marriage build or increase over time?

What keeps you from initiating intimacy with your husband?

In what ways is your intimate relationship with your husband dependent on your intimate relationship with God?

THE UNVEILED WIFE

MATTHEW 27:50-51, 2 CORINTHIANS 3:16-18,

PROVERBS 3:5-6

On a warm summer day in July, a crowd gathered at the top of a hillside. A Pastor ushered four men in black suits toward a canopy trimmed in garland. The murmurs of the guests silenced as the procession was queued. Covered in a elegant blanket of white, the bride made her way gracefully down the aisle. Family and friends were excited to celebrate such a joyous occasion, their eyes twinkling in admiration and delight following her every step. Hints of the bride's elation shone through her veil which draped down to her shoulders. Although feeling blessed by the support of all who showed up, the veil served as a shield of protection, as if it was something she could hide behind, making it easier for her to walk through the parted sea of people. Her focus was narrowed in on the man waiting for her hand at the altar, her desire was marriage.

As the ceremony progressed, it came time for the unveiling of the bride. Reaching his hands gently toward the rim of silk trimming the veil, the groom lifted it from her face and softly placed it over her hair. Beauty radiated from the bride as she became revealed before her husband. He could see her now more clearly, more closely, more intimately. To the bride, the unveiling symbolized that it was finished, the wedding ceremony and everything they had endured up to this point was finished--they were officially married, pronounced husband and wife, and their life together as one was just beginning.

There was another powerful unveiling that took place which also had quite a lot of symbolism. When Jesus died on the cross, at that moment when He took His last breath, the curtain of the temple was torn in two. This particular curtain in the temple had previously been a barrier between man and God, a chasm brought on by the sin of man. The symbolism of it tearing represented the reconciliation that Christ provided through His sacrifice. By accepting Jesus Christ as Lord and Savior, man now had a way to have a personal relationship with God. In Christ the veil is lifted.

When you accept Jesus into your heart as Lord and Savior, there is a moment of unveiling in your heart, where the walls that seemed to protect you from the world are let down so that the Holy Spirit may come in and dwell, and not just dwell, but transform you into the image of God, the woman He created you to be.

Being unveiled is an intimate experience because you are exposing yourself, you are exposing your heart. In an intimate relationship you cannot remain hidden and shielded from the one who desires to know you. You must lift the veil, you must be transparent and honest, you must make yourself known, fully known. In doing so you will experience extraordinary.

Being unveiled is not a one-time event at the altar, whether you are getting married or marrying Christ. Being unveiled is a posture, an attitude of the heart where humility abounds. Being unveiled is a process of revealing yourself to another, motivated by pure love. Being unveiled is one of the most beautiful, precious, and priceless feelings you will ever encounter.

Wherever you are, whatever circumstance you are facing, know that you are not alone in your struggles. God yearns to help you through this journey. Always trust in His truth, always lean on His understanding, and always submit to Him, and He will make your paths straight. God is your source of power and strength. He is the only one who is capable of fulfilling you completely. Unveil yourself to Him and He will transform you. He will also be your help so that you can unveil yourself to your husband. May you continually walk in His amazing grace, covered in a blanket of pure white.

Dear Lord,

Please help me to be unveiled before You and before my husband. I am becoming more aware of the need to make myself fully known to You and to my husband. As I remain unveiled, please transform me and help me embrace Your role for me as a wife. Thank You so much for caring about me in such great ways. I love You, God! I am so thankful that You sent Your Son so I could be set free! I pray that I am an unveiled wife, a wife who continually seeks after You! I pray that I would be transparent in my relationship with my husband, that I would be willing to share my whole heart, without holding anything back. Please fill me with Your courage and Your truth. The enemy is so good at infusing my heart with lies, convincing me to hide, convincing me to remain isolated and broken, convincing me that I am not good enough to radiate Christ. I claim freedom. May Your Holy Spirit write Your truth on my heart so much that there would be no room for any lies. May Your precious will be done in me and through me.

In Jesus' name, AMEN!

Challenge:
Memorize 2 Corinthians 3:16-18. Also, pray and ask God to help you be unveiled.

Status Update:
"@unveiledwife I am an Unveiled Wife!" #WifeAfterGod

Questions:
Why is it important for you to be unveiled in your intimate relationships?

What things keep you from being unveiled?

What is one step you can take to be unveiled before God, as well as with your husband?

LOVE LETTER TO HUSBAND

PROVERBS 31:11-12, COLOSSIANS 3:12-17, 1 JOHN 4:7-12

As you draw closer to God, growth in your marriage is inevitable. God's truth is too powerful to not make any ripple at all. The transformation you encounter with God changes the very threads which weave your heart together. Character traits such as compassion, kindness, humility, gentleness, and patience become foundational pillars defining your every action. God's love will radiate from you so beautifully others will notice your glow. Draw close to God and you will draw closer to your husband. These are the two most important relationships you will ever encounter and they are the ministry to which you have been called to serve. May you go forth with passion and endurance to fulfill God's will for your life as a daughter of the Most High and as a wonderful wife.

This parting chapter is a call to action, a challenge to take all that you have learned from the previous chapters and implement them into your life, especially in your role as a wife. Begin with a letter to your husband. Before you write it out, pray over it and ask God to inspire the words you should share with your husband. Perhaps it is a letter of affirmation, perhaps it is a letter of confession, or perhaps it is a song declaring your great love for him. It could even be a collection of many different things. The goal is to share your heart with your husband, to be wide-open, honest and unveiled.

Before you decide when to give your husband the letter, pray over it. Ask God when you should gift it to him and how you should present it. Maybe you will go on a hike together or maybe a nice dinner out. This is a challenge for you to rely on God, to listen to Him, and to experience how He leads you. Once you have the written letter, pray about when you should give it and how. Then, with courage in your heart, present it to your husband.

You are a wife after God. Continue to seek after Him daily. Continue to seek peace and pursue it. Continue to love and respect your husband. You are beautiful, you are worthy, and your purpose is great. You are a wife after God!

May your marriage experience extraordinary!

The encouragement you received on this journey does not need to just stop and be left forgotten about. Keep it close to your heart, revisit it often, venture to execute the challenges again and again and share its impact with others.

Dear Lord,

I am in awe of how You spoke to me throughout this devotional. I value every word that You inspired and I was encouraged along the way. I pray over this last challenge. Please speak to me about what I should share in my letter to my husband. Holy Spirit may You guide my heart. I am listening and watching to see how You respond. I also pray for a creative way to present this letter, a way that would be meaningful to my husband. May You use this letter to bless him and bless our marriage.

In Jesus' name, AMEN!

Challenge:

After you give your husband your letter, write down what resulted from the experience.

Also, please take a moment to visit unveiledwife.com/letter-to-my-husband and if you desire, submit your letter to your husband, you can do this anonymously or leave your name. Your letter will encourage other wives looking for inspiration on how to unveil their hearts and it will be a testament of the power of God working in your life, a testament for others to be encouraged by.

Status Update:

"@unveiledwife By God's grace I will experience an extraordinary marriage." #WifeAfterGod

Questions:

What was the hardest thing about this last challenge?

What are other affectionate gestures you could do to draw closer to your husband?

DID YOU KNOW THAT THERE IS A
COMPANION DEVOTIONAL
FOR YOUR HUSBAND?

GET IT TODAY AT
HUSBANDAFTERGOD.COM

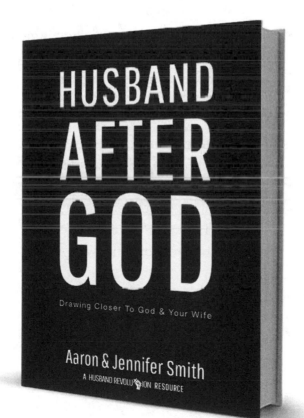

If this devotional has impacted your faith and marriage please let me know by posting a testimony here:
WifeAfterGod.com

For more marriage resources please visit:
unveiledwife.com/marriage-resources/

Recieve daily prayer for your marriage via email:
unveiledwife.com/daily-prayer/

Get connected:
Facebook.com/unveiledwife
Pinterest.com/unveiledwife
Youtube.com/unveiledwife
Instagram.com/unveiledwife
Twitter.com/unveiledwife

Interested in leading a group study?
WivesAfterGod.com